access to history

in depth

ANTI-SEMITISM
and the HOLOCAUST

Alan Farmer

Hodder & Stoughton

A MEMBER OF THE HODDER HEADLINE GROUP

Order queries: please contact Bookpoint Ltd, 39 Milton Park, Abingdon, Oxon OX14 4TD. Telephone: (44) 01235 400414, Fax (44) 01235 400454. Lines are open from 9.00 - 6.00, Monday to Saturday, with a 24 hour message answering service. Email address: orders@bookpoint.co.uk

British Library Cataloguing in Publication Data

A catalogue for this title is available from the British Library

ISBN 0 340 69793 8

First published 1998

Impression number	10	9	8	7	6	5	4	3	2
Year			2002	2001	2000	1999	1998		

Cover photo from The Institute of Contemporary History and the Wiener Library Ltd, London.

Illustrations by Ian Foulis & Associates Ltd, Saltash
Typeset by Sempringham publishing services, Bedford
Printed in Great Britain for Hodder & Stoughton Educational,
a division of Hodder Headline Plc, 338 Euston Road, London NW1 3BH
by Redwood Books, Trowbridge, Wiltshire.

Contents

Acknowledgements

The photograph on the front cover was taken at the liberation of Buchenwald in 1945 and is reproduced courtesy of The Institute of Contemporary History and the Wiener Library Ltd, London.

The publishers would like to thank the following for permission to reproduce the following copyright illustrations:
   Bundesarchiv, p. 42; © copyright Steidl Verlag, Göttingen 1989, page 62 top and bottom and page 63 top and bottom; Yad Vashem Museum, Jerusalem, Israel page 85 top and bottom.

The Publishers would like to thank the following for permission to reproduce material in this volume:
   Constable and Co. for an extract from *Nazi Germany: A New History* by KP Fischer (1995); Edward Arnold for an extract from *Hitler and the Jews: The Genesis of the Holocaust* by Philippe Burrin (1989); Gazelle Book Services Ltd for extracts from *Encyclopedia of the Third Reich* by Louis L Synder (1976); History Review for an extract from 'The Decision to Kill the Jews' by I Kershaw (*History Review* no. 12, 1992); University of Exeter Press for extracts from *Nazism 1919-1945 vol 2: State, Economy and Society 1933-1939* edited by J Noakes and G Pridham (1984) and for extracts from *Nazism 1919-1945 vol 3: Foreign Policy, War and Racial Extermination* edited by J Noakes and G Pridham (1988); AP Watt Ltd on behalf of Sir Gilbert Martin CBE for permission to reproduce two maps from *The Holocaust: A History of the Jews in Europe during the Second World War* (Rinehart and Winston, 1985).

Every effort has been made to trace and acknowledge ownership of copyright. The publishers will be glad to make suitable arrangements with any copyright holders whom it has not been possible to contact.

Preface

The original *Access to History* series was conceived as a collection of sets of books covering popular chronological periods in British history, such as 'The Tudors' and 'the nineteenth century', together with the histories of other countries, such as France, Germany, Russia and the USA. This arrangement complemented the way in which early-modern and modern history has traditionally been taught in sixth forms, colleges and universities. In recent years, however, other ways of dividing up the past have become increasingly popular. In particular, there has been a greater emphasis on studying relatively brief periods in considerable detail and on comparing similar historical phenomena in different countries. These developments have generated a demand for appropriate learning materials, and, in response, two new 'strands' are being added to the main series - *In Depth* and *Themes*. The new volumes build directly on the features that have made *Access to History* so popular.

To the general reader

Although *Access* books have been specifically designed to meet the needs of examination students, these volumes also have much to offer the general reader. *Access* authors are committed to the belief that good history must not only be accurate, up-to-date and scholarly, but also clearly and attractively written. The main body of the text (excluding the 'Study Guides') should, therefore, form a readable and engaging survey of a topic. Moreover, each author has aimed not merely to provide as clear an explanation as possible of what happened in the past but also to stimulate readers and to challenge them into thinking for themselves about the past and its significance. Thus, although no prior knowledge is expected from the reader, he or she is treated as an intelligent and thinking person throughout. The author tends to share ideas and explore possibilities, instead of delivering so-called 'historical truths' from on high.

To the student reader

It is intended that *Access* books should be used by students studying history at a higher level. Its volumes are all designed to be working texts, which should be reasonably clear on a first reading but which will benefit from re-reading and close study. To be an effective and successful student, you need to budget your time wisely. Hence you should think carefully about how important the material in a particular book is for you. If you simply need to acquire a general grasp of a topic, the following approach will probably be effective:

   I. Read Chapter 1, which should give you an overview of the whole book, and think about its contents.

2. Skim through Chapter 2, paying particular attention to the opening section and to the headings and sub-headings. Decide if you need to read the whole chapter.
3. If you do, read the chapter, stopping at the end of every sub-division of the text to make notes.
4. Repeat stage 2 (and stage 3 where appropriate) for the other chapters.

If, however, your course - and your particular approach to it - demands a detailed knowledge of the contents of the book, you will need to be correspondingly more thorough. There is no perfect way of studying, and it is particularly worthwhile experimenting with different styles of note-making to find the one that best suits you. Nevertheless, the following plan of action is worth trying:

1. Read a whole chapter quickly, preferably at one sitting. Avoid the temptation - which may be very great - to make notes at this stage.
2. Study the flow diagram at the end of the chapter, ensuring that you understand the general 'shape' of what you have read.
3. Re-read the chapter more slowly, this time taking notes. You may well be amazed at how much more intelligible and straightforward the material seems on a second reading - and your notes will be correspondingly more useful to you when you have to write an essay or revise for an exam. In the long run, reading a chapter twice can, in fact, often save time. Be sure to make your notes in a clear, orderly fashion, and spread them out so that, if necessary, you can later add extra information.
4. Read the advice on essay questions, and do tackle the specimen titles. (Remember that if learning is to be effective, it must be active. No one - alas - has yet devised any substitute for real effort. It is up to you to make up your own mind on the key issues in any topic.)
5. Attempt the source-based questions. The guidance on tackling these exercises, which is generally given at least once in a book, is well worth reading and thinking about.

When you have finished the main chapters, go through the 'Further Reading' section. Remember that no single book can ever do more than introduce a topic, and it is to be hoped that - time permitting - you will want to read more widely. If *Access* books help you to discover just how diverse and fascinating the human past can be, the series will have succeeded in its aim - and you will experience that enthusiasm for the subject which, along with efficient learning, is the hallmark of all the best students.

Robert Pearce

1 The Holocaust: the Historiographical Debates

1 Introduction

This book is an attempt to explain the persecution - and ultimately mass killing - of German and European Jews which occurred in the 1930s and 1940s and which is associated with Adolf Hitler and the Nazi Party. By the end of 1941 Hitler was, almost certainly, committed to a plan to murder all the Jews living in territory either directly controlled by Germany or in the German sphere of influence. (By 1941 this meant most of Europe.) This genocidal plan (genocide is the deliberate extermination of a race) came to fruition in 1942 and continued until 1945. The systematic attempt to exterminate all European Jews is usually referred to as the Final Solution or the Holocaust. Neither term is entirely satisfactory. 'Final Solution' was used by the Nazis before 1941 to describe whichever anti-Jewish policy was in vogue at the time. Consequently there were several 'final solutions' (which did not involve the annihilation of the Jews) before the final 'Final Solution'. The word Holocaust comes from a third century BC Greek edition of the Old Testament, translating as 'the burnt sacrificial offering dedicated exclusively to God'. While Israeli historians have sometimes preferred to use the Hebrew word 'Shoah' (meaning destruction), this book will use both Holocaust and Final Solution interchangeably simply because they are the terms most commonly used in the English-speaking world.

Many think the word Holocaust should refer exclusively to the fate of the Jews, thus emphasising the distinctiveness of the Jewish experience. However, the Jews were not the first and by no means the only group of people to be slaughtered by the Nazis. In 1939 Hitler's government embarked on the so-called euthanasia programme - a euphemism to camouflage the mass murder of Germany's physically and mentally handicapped. Some 70,000 people deemed 'unworthy of life' had been killed by August 1941, before the Final Solution was really underway. During the course of the Second World War, the Nazis killed large numbers of people because of their national origins (e.g. Poles and Russians), their behaviour (e.g. criminals and homosexuals), their political affiliations (e.g. socialists and communists) and because of their activities in the war (e.g. Soviet prisoners of war). The Holocaust cannot be understood except in terms of the killing of these other groups.

But most historians accept that the Jewish suffering was worse than that of any other group, except perhaps the Gypsies who were also murdered because they were perceived to be a biologically defined group. The killing of most of the other victims lacked the co-ordinated 'spiritual' zeal that the Nazis reserved for the Jews. The essence of the Holocaust was the fact that it targeted every Jew for death.

It is impossible to give an exact figure for the number of Jews killed. The Nazis themselves had difficulties defining who exactly was Jewish and were not always certain which victims were Jewish and which were non-Jewish. Nor is it clear how many Jews lived in Europe pre-1941 or how many were still alive post-1945. The accuracy of statistics varies from country to country. Perhaps the greatest difficulty is establishing the number of deaths in the USSR. The Russian archives have only recently been opened to western scholars and there is still massive research work to do. While the Nazis recorded some portions of the Final Solution with great accuracy, at other times little was recorded - or has survived. Given the problems with the evidence, the debate about the precise numbers killed looks set to continue. However, most historians accept the findings of the War Crimes Tribunal at Nuremberg in 1946 and agree that some five to six million Jews died in the years 1941-5 - one third of the world's Jewish population. The murder of the Jews was carried out largely outside Germany. Over one million were shot by execution squads in the USSR. Some four million were gassed or worked to death in camps in Poland. By 1942 the killing was on an industrial scale as Jews from every corner of Europe were deported eastwards to die. While there have been many instances of concentrated persecution of Jews throughout history, the sheer magnitude of the Holocaust makes it a unique and terrible event.

Whether the Holocaust was the most horrendous crime of the twentieth century - the ultimate standard of evil against which all other degrees of evil should be measured - is debatable. Probably Stalin (in the USSR) and Mao zedung (in China) killed more people in the name of economic determinism than Hitler killed in the name of racial determinism. Nevertheless, given that the Holocaust was one of the worst lapses into barbarism in the world's history, it is difficult to discuss rationally. In the 1980s there was talk, especially in Germany, that the subject was so horrendous and so totally beyond human comprehension that it could not be adequately dealt with by historians. This view was always silly. As historian Yehuda Bauer says: 'if the Holocaust was caused by humans and its horrors inflicted on other humans and watched by yet other groups of humans, then it is as understandable as any other historical event'.[1] Historians cannot and should not avoid dealing with the subject. To suppress it would not just be a crime against history but also a crime against those who died.

There are still some people who claim that the Holocaust did not happen. Over the years the 'deniers' have encompassed a wide spectrum of beliefs. Paul Rassinier, a French socialist who survived the horrors of two German concentration camps, was one of the first to claim that the gas chambers did not exist - largely because he had not seen one. Rassinier's case rested essentially on conviction: he did little research to substantiate it. His general view was that the Holocaust was a myth created by American and Jewish capitalists to help the birth of the state of Israel. Right-wing 'deniers', by contrast, have tended to the view that the Holocaust was a myth created by Jews and communists to damn the Nazis. They stress that much of the evidence for the Holocaust comes from the USSR and that no record emanating from the USSR in the 1940s can be trusted. It is conceivable that the USSR, for propaganda purposes, could have 'invented' the Holocaust. However, the 'deniers' case collapses because there is colossal evidence, not only from surviving Jews but also from the German perpetrators themselves - memoirs, eyewitness reports, court testimonies, official government documents - that the Holocaust did occur. So overwhelming is this evidence that to deny the existence of the Holocaust is ludicrous.

Over the last 50 years, historians from many countries - Israel, the USA, Britain and Germany, in particular - have produced detailed analyses of the persecution and liquidation of European Jewry. The deportation and extermination process is not really subject to dispute among serious researchers. However, many critical questions about the Holocaust remain.

This book can do little more than touch the surface of some of them.

2 To What Extent Was Adolf Hitler to Blame?

For nearly two decades after 1945 it was generally assumed that Hitler was totally responsible for the Holocaust - and everything else that happened in Nazi Germany. The Third Reich was seen as a monolithic state where all power was concentrated in the Führer's hands. Hitler's vitriolic hatred of all Jews was seen as sufficient on its own to explain the murder of millions of Jews. Many historians (they are often referred to as 'intentionalists') still believe that Hitler was an all-powerful dictator whose will was invariably translated into action. Some intentionalists (like Lucy Dawidowicz) see him conceiving the idea of the extermination of the Jews in the 1920s and pursuing this intention remorselessly once he came to power in 1933. In the intentionalists' opinion Hitler's domestic and foreign policies were dictated by the determination to purify and strengthen the German race. Internally, Germany was to be improved by weeding out those held to be racially undesirable - Jews, Gypsies and the handicapped. Externally, foreign conquest would secure *lebensraum* (or living space). The attack on the USSR in June 1941 was, in the intentionalists' view, a deliberate attempt to win *lebensraum* and eliminate Jews.

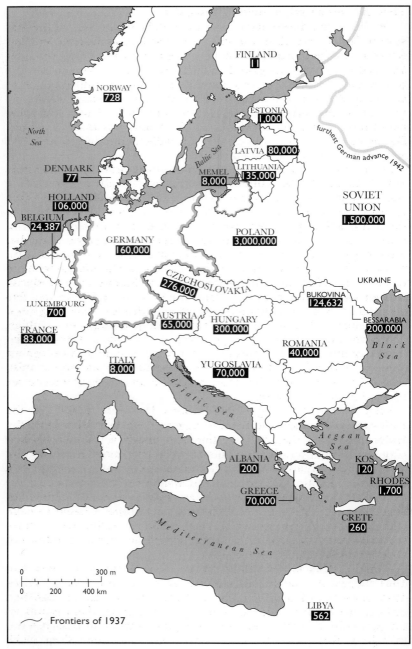

Martin Gilbert's estimates of Jews murdered between 1 September 1939 and 8 May 1945

They thus see a straight road to Auschwitz.

Few historians doubt that racism and anti-Semitism were at the very core of Hitler's creed. In the same way that Karl Marx believed class struggle was the motive force behind the historical process, so Hitler believed it was race struggle. Perceiving the Jews as the source of all evil in the world, Hitler was committed to eliminating them from Germany. But what did elimination mean? Did it mean mass slaughter - or simply mass deportation? And did Hitler have clear ideas about how 'elimination' (whatever this meant) was to be achieved? Did he have fixed strategies or did he usually tend to improvise? And was he really an all-powerful dictator?

Some historians (they are often called 'structuralists' or 'functionalists') doubt whether Hitler was the superman Führer depicted by Nazi propaganda. Functionalists stress that Hitler was not always free to act as he wished. Nor did he initiate every major development in the Third Reich. His power was restricted in a number of ways, not least by the sheer impossibility of one man controlling everything that was going on in a country of over 70 million people - and soon to grow considerably. Moreover, functionalists think that Hitler's government was far from efficient. The research of Hans Mommsen and Martin Broszat suggests that Nazi Germany bore more resemblance to a feudal than a modern twentieth-century state, with great Nazi 'magnates' (like Heinrich Himmler and Herman Goering) engaged in a ruthless and never-ending power struggle to capture the 'king' (Hitler), who in turn maintained his authority by playing one great lord off against another. Virtually all functionalists see Hitler as an opportunist, responding to events rather than taking the initiative, and some see him as lazy and indecisive.

Such a view has major implications for Hitler's role in the Holocaust. Mommsen and Broszat suggest that Hitler drifted into the Holocaust rather than it being the final phase of a long-cherished plan. They point out that the pressure of events and the influence of powerful individuals all had a major influence on him. They also look within the chaotic Nazi government system itself for at least some explanation for the Holocaust and claim that it was largely initiated by local Nazi authorities in occupied eastern Europe. Unable to cope with the masses of Jews under their control, these authorities (according to Mommsen) came up with improvised murderous solutions in different places at different times.

Functionalists believe that Hitler's actions between 1933 and 1941 suggest that he was not necessarily intent on mass murder. By 1940 more than half of the Jews in Germany and Austria had fled or been driven out. This was an odd policy to adopt if Hitler was set on genocide. Nor was there any immediate mass killing of the two million Polish Jews who came under German control in 1939. Thus, it is possible to argue that the road to Auschwitz was 'twisted'[2] and that the Holocaust was not the inevitable result of

Hitler's coming to power in 1933.

However, functionalist historians have recently been severely criticised. One major charge is that they have focused to such a degree upon the administrative arrangements in the Third Reich that they have lost sight of the motive force and ideological climate which informed the decisions. Most Holocaust historians today believe that Hitler was very much at the centre - and in control - of events rather than simply one of a cast of thousands, ad libbing his way through an unscripted drama. 'In all its major decisions', declares Saul Friedländer, 'the [Nazi] regime depended on Hitler'.[3] While he sometimes only intervened spasmodically, there seems plenty of evidence to suggest that he could send orders crashing through the system like bolts of lightning to ensure his will was carried out. Yet while accepting Hitler's ultimate responsibility, anti-functionalist historians disagree about when, how and in what circumstances the Holocaust order was given. Did Hitler set the objective - get rid of Jews - without specifying how this was to be achieved? Did he give one or a series of orders which finally culminated in the Holocaust? Did he give the order(s) before or after the launch of Operation Barbarossa? Did his decision(s) result from the triumphalist atmosphere of mid-summer 1941, when German victory over the USSR seemed inevitable? Or did the decision(s) emerge only towards the end of 1941, when hopes of a quick victory had been dashed?

In 1977 the right-wing historian David Irving asserted that Hitler only learned of the Holocaust on 7 October 1943. He offered a £1,000 reward to anyone who could produce a wartime document proving that Hitler knew about the Final Solution before that date.[4] Irving's many critics (which include both intentionalists and functionalists) point out that he conveniently ignored Hitler's hate-filled rhetoric about Jews. They also stress that written orders were not necessary to begin the killing process. Hitler rarely committed himself to paper and preferred to give his orders orally. The lack of written orders from Hitler is, in essence, the problem. Given this situation, historians are likely to continue to disagree about Hitler's precise role in the Holocaust.

3 How Responsible Were Himmler, Heydrich and the SS?

Heinrich Himmler, head of the *Schutzstaffel* (or SS), ensured that Hitler's orders were carried out. An extreme racist who was totally loyal to Hitler, Himmler is often regarded (for example, by Richard Breitman) as the 'architect of genocide'.[5] However, Himmler delegated considerable authority in Jewish matters to Reinhard Heydrich, his loyal henchman. At the Wannsee conference in January 1942 it was Heydrich who formalised the administrative arrangements of the

Holocaust. The SS, a highly organised police apparatus, was a perfect instrument for genocide. Its members were fanatical Nazis and had a grossly distorted sense of duty. Few doubt that Himmler, Heydrich and the SS played a vital role in the Final Solution. However, Himmler and Heydrich were not the only leading Nazis involved in anti-Jewish initiatives. Nor were the SS the only killers. To what extent have the SS become Germany's whipping boys - a useful alibi for many other groups and individuals? To what extent did Himmler and/or Heydrich play a determining role in the Holocaust?

4 What Was the Extent of the Euthanasia Connection?

Recently historians like Henry Friedländer and Michael Burleigh have pointed out the connection between the euthanasia killings and the Holocaust. The ideology, the decision-making process, the personnel and the killing technique all seem to tie the euthanasia programme to the Final Solution. Should the euthanasia programme be considered separately to genocide? Or was it, as Friedländer claims, 'the first chapter'?[6]

5 How Guilty Was the German Army?

It was once claimed that the German armed forces (the *Wehrmacht*) were untainted by Hitler's racism and not responsible for the Holocaust. After 1945 many of Germany's top officers claimed they were unaware of what was happening to the Jews. Most historians now, however, believe that the army was massively implicated in the Final Solution. German historians like Christian Streit and Jürgen Forster have argued that the bulk of leading *Wehrmacht* officers were anti-Bolshevik and anti-Semitic and, regarding the war against the USSR as a war to the death, were quite content to support the brutality of the SS. The letters and diaries of ordinary German troops suggest that the majority were also extremely racist. Many seem to have carried out horrendous massacres with enthusiasm. To what extent was the *Wehrmacht* an active - and willing - participant in the Holocaust?

6 To What Extent Were the German People Responsible?

After 1945 most Germans insisted they had no idea of what was happening to Jews in the east. Many may have been telling the truth. There is no doubt that the Holocaust was implemented with the utmost secrecy. However, Hitler, Himmler and the Nazi elite did not act alone. Their decisions had to be accepted and their policies implemented by many others. Precisely how many others is a subject of heated debate. Recent research has tended to contradict the notion that Germans knew little about what was going on. Many years ago Raul Hilberg suggested that large numbers of Germans - civil servants, railway workers, policemen - were involved in what he termed the 'machinery of destruction'. More recently Daniel Goldhagen has argued that the German people were not simply cogs in a vast apparatus beyond their control. He has also claimed that most Germans supported the policy of mass murder and that between 100,000 and 500,000 Germans were directly implicated in it. With so many involved, the question Goldhagen asks is: how could the German people subsequently plead such total ignorance? He also asserts that: 'The notion that ordinary Danes or Italians would have acted as the ordinary Germans did strains credulity beyond the breaking point'.[7]

In terms of trying to reach a conclusion about the collective responsibility of the Germans for the Holocaust, several questions have to be answered. How anti-Semitic were most Germans? How many people knew what was going on in the east? How many were implicated in - and to what extent was there widespread support for - the Holocaust?

7 Was European Anti-Semitism to Blame?

Anti-Semitism was a European - and not just a German - phenomenon. For over a thousand years no century has passed without Jews being persecuted and killed in some part of Europe. In the 1930s several countries in eastern Europe passed legislation discriminating against Jews. Violence against Jews was particularly widespread in Poland. Jewish shops and houses were frequently attacked and scores of Polish Jews killed in pogroms. Even Polish church leaders expressed anti-Semitic views. After 1939, according to many Israeli historians, the Polish people as a whole showed little sympathy to the Jews - and some supported Nazi actions against them. In those areas of the USSR occupied by the Germans after 1941, local people - Lithuanians, Estonians and Ukrainians - frequently co-operated with the Germans in slaughtering Jews. Romanian troops murdered thousands of Jews in 1941-2. Moreover, many of Germany's allies and client states in western and central Europe - not least France - collaborated with the Nazis and agreed that their Jews should be deported eastwards. It can thus be claimed that 'ordinary' Germans acted no differently from 'ordinary' Romanians, Lithuanians and a host of other European groups who also became Hitler's 'willing executioners'. To what extent did European anti-Semitism contribute to the Holocaust?

8 Did Jews Collaborate in Their Own Destruction?

In 1963 the Jewish scholar Hannah Arendt claimed that: 'if the Jewish people had really been unorganised and leaderless, there would have been chaos and plenty of misery but the total number of victims would hardly have been between four and a half and six million people'.[8] Arendt (and before her Raul Hilberg) charged Jewish leaders with helping the process of destruction by complying with Nazi orders to supply names and groups of Jews for transportation to the death camps. Many scholars have rejected this thesis. Isaiah Trunk, for example, focused attention on the dilemma confronting Jewish leaders in the Polish ghettos. His conclusion was that they were in an impossible position. Having little option but to obey Nazi commands, they did their best to protect their communities. But could and should there have been more Jewish resistance?

9 To What Extent Were America, Britain and the Papacy to Blame?

Could the western Allies have done more to save European Jewry? The extreme view, propounded by Arthur Morse and David Wyman, is that the USA and Britain shared responsibility for the Holocaust. Morse and Wyman castigated both countries for having restrictive immigration policies with regard to Jews in the 1930s. Would-be Jewish refugees, unable to settle in Palestine (then a British mandate) or the USA, consequently died in the Nazi death camps. Morse and Wyman also argued that President Roosevelt and Winston Churchill could have done far more to assist the Jews during the war.

But other historians (for example, William Rubenstein) think the idea of Allied complicity in the Holocaust is a gross distortion of historical fact. Given that Britain and the USA had no idea what Hitler intended ultimately to do, they cannot be blamed for restricting Jewish immigration in the 1930s. Arguably once war broke out, there was little the Allied governments could do to help the Jews. Most Jews were murdered in 1942 - at a time when Hitler controlled most of continental Europe and before the Allies were aware of the full scale of the Holocaust. Allied leaders decided it was impossible to consider making any kind of deal with Hitler and determined that the best way to help the Jews was to win the war as quickly as possible. But was this the right policy?

Could the Christian churches have done more to help the Jews? The silence of Pope Pius X11 - who said nothing in condemnation of the Holocaust - has been criticised by many historians. Might moral pressure from the Church have had some impact on German and Austrian public opinion?

References

1 Yehuda Bauer, 'Conclusion: The significance of the Final Solution', in David Cesarini (ed), *The Final Solution: Origins and Implementation* (Routledge, 1994), p.303.

2 Karl Schleunes, *The Twisted Road to Auschwitz: Nazi Policy towards German Jews 1933-1939* (Deutsch, 1970).

3 Saul Friedländer, *Nazi Germany and the Jews: The Years of Persecution 1933-39* (Weidenfeld and Nicolson, 1997), p. 3.

4 David Irving, *Hitler's War* (Viking, 1977).

5 Richard Breitman, *The Architect of Genocide: Himmler and the Final Solution* (The Bodley Head, 1991).

6 Henry Friedländer, *The Origins of Nazi Genocide: From Euthanasia to the Final Solution* (The University of North Carolina Press, 1995), p. 8.

7 Daniel J. Goldhagen, *Hitler's Willing Executioners: Ordinary Germans and the Holocaust* (Little, Brown and Company, 1996), p. 408

8 Hannah Arendt, *Eichmann in Jerusalem: A Report on the Banality of Evil* (Viking, 1963), pp. 110-111.

Summary Diagram
The Holocaust: the Historiographical Debates

Hitler's responsibility?

How many died?

Himmler and the SS. Architects or whipping boys?

The Holocaust. Areas of debate

European responsibility?

Allied responsibility?

Euthanasia connection?

Papal responsibility?

Collective guilt of German people?

German Army involvement?

2 Anti-Semitism and Nazism

1 Introduction

'Was there any form of filth or crime without at least one Jew involved in it? If you cut into such a sore, you find, like a maggot in a rotting body, often dazzled by the sudden light - a Jew.'[1] So wrote Adolf Hitler in the mid-1920s. Hitler's anti-Jewish views were by no means original and by no means unique to him. Arguably he was the product rather than the creator of an anti-Semitic society. Anti-Semitism pervaded many aspects of German life in the late-nineteenth and early-twentieth centuries. This helps explain the political success of Hitler and the Nazi Party in the early 1930s. Once Hitler came to power in 1933, it was inevitable that some anti-Jewish action would be taken. This chapter will first consider the roots of anti-Semitism, especially in Germany. It will go on to examine Hitler's own ideology, and conclude by examining the nature of Hitler's rule - which is highly relevant to what happened to Jews after 1933.

2 The Roots of Anti-Semitism

Anti-Semitism, far from being confined to Germany, had deep roots in Europe generally. It varied in intensity in different countries and at different times. In the Middle Ages, European anti-Semitism was based to a large extent on religious hostility: the Jews were blamed for the death of Christ and for not accepting Christianity. For centuries it was virtually impossible to be Christian without being anti-Semitic. Jews were also unpopular as money-lenders at a time when charging interest for loans was banned by the Christian Church. In medieval Europe, Jews were likely to be segregated in ghettos, face forcible expulsion from countries (they were driven from England in 1290), and liable to face violent assault and the destruction of their property. Riotous outbreaks against Jews were known as pogroms. In spite - or possibly because - of the persecution they suffered, most Jews retained a strong identity, regardless of the country in which they lived. This ensured they remained as 'outsiders' and potential scapegoats.

In the late eighteenth and early nineteenth centuries, however, many western European states accepted Jews as citizens with the same rights as everybody else and made efforts to integrate them into society. Most Jews welcomed this and quickly accepted the social norms and values of the nations in which they lived. While anti-Semitism did not disappear in western Europe, hostility towards Jews, in Germany and elsewhere, was generally politically insignificant by the mid-nineteenth century. In 1871 the new German empire extended total civil equality to Jews.

Yet in many parts of eastern Europe, where there were large Jewish minorities, anti-Semitism remained strong. Throughout the nine-teenth century, thousands of eastern European Jews moved west-wards, often settling in Germany and Austria-Hungary where there was far less discrimination and far more economic opportunity. At first most Jewish emigrants found themselves at the bottom of the economic pile, but many benefited from the processes of industriali-sation and urbanisation. By the 1870s some two-thirds of German Jews had managed to rise into the middle and upper taxation levels and a (disproportionate) number became doctors, lawyers and academics. By 1900 Jews played an active and visible part in the cultural, economic and financial life of Germany. Most saw themselves as loyal Germans. Many no longer identified with a separate Jewish commu-nity, and some inter-married with Germans and became converts to Christianity. It was a similar story in Austria.

3 Racial Anti-Semitism

However, just as it seemed as though Jews were being assimilated into European society, new anti-Semitic tendencies were developing. While there had probably always been a racial aspect to anti-Jewish feeling, prior to the nineteenth century anti-Semitism had been mainly religious. During the late nineteenth century it became increasingly racial. Early in the century, a growing interest in race had led numbers of European academics to try to define race and cate-gorise racial characteristics. In the mid-1850s, the Frenchman Count Joseph Arthur de Gobineau produced a work entitled *Essay on the Inequality of Human Races*, in which he argued that different races were physically and psychologically different. History, in Gobineau's view, was essentially a race struggle and the rise and fall of civilisations was racially determined. All the high cultures in the world were the work of the 'Aryan' (which equated with, but was not quite the same as, the 'Germanic') race. Cultures declined, he claimed, when the Aryan ruling caste interbred with members of 'racially less valuable' lower orders.

Charles Darwin's *Origin of Species*, published in 1859, provided further ammunition for the race cause. Darwin himself said nothing about racial theories: his book was concerned with plants and animals. But his theory of natural selection as the means of evolution was adopted - and adapted - by many scholars. 'Social Darwinists' were soon claiming that races and nations needed to be fit to survive and rule. Some went further and argued that a nation's most important political task was to eliminate all those who were racially weak or harmful, and to cultivate only those who were racially strong and useful.

Many late nineteenth century European writers extolled the virtues of the Aryan, Teutonic or Germanic races. These same writers were often anti-Semitic, finding fault not just with the Jews' religious beliefs but with their biology as well.

Anti-Semitism in Germany in the second half of the nineteenth century became associated with the rise of militant nationalism. Large numbers of German nationalists accepted that the Germans were indeed the master race and had an almost mystical faith in the *Volk*. (The word translates as people or 'folk', but the concept went beyond that.) The superiority of the German *Volk* was seen as arising from a sense of community based on ancestral blood ties. The *Volk* was seen as preserving the warrior virtues - honour, duty, courage and loyalty - of Germanic society. German nationalists, while extolling their 'blood community', were invariably hostile to - and contemptuous of - other races, especially the Jews. Jews came to stand for all that the *volkisch* ideologues loathed - liberalism, socialism, pacifism and modernism.

A host of late nineteenth century German scholars helped make anti-Semitism fashionable and respectable. In 1881 the economist Eugen Dühring, for example, argued that the feelings, thinking and behaviour of human beings was racially determined, and claimed that the 'scarcely human' Jews were the enemies of all nations, but especially the enemies of Germany. In 1887 the philosopher Paul de Lagarde described Jews as 'vermin' and asserted that there was a need for a 'surgical incision' to 'remove the source of infection'.[2] Pamphleteers, newspaper editors and politicians presented anti-Semitic views to the German public. So did artists and musicians. Richard Wagner, the famous composer, was particularly nationalistic and anti-Semitic.

Among the most prominent anti-Semitic writers was Wagner's son-in-law, Houston Stewart Chamberlain. Son of a British admiral and a German mother, Chamberlain published his most influential work - *Foundations of the Nineteenth Century* - in 1899. Chamberlain argued that the Jews were a degenerate, evil race, conspiring to attain world domination and threatening German greatness. He saw the struggle between Jews and Germans as the central theme of world history: 'Where the struggle is not waged with cannon-balls, it goes on silently in the heart of society ... But this struggle, silent though it be, is above all a struggle for life and death.'[3] His book became an immediate best-seller and even drew praise from Kaiser Wilhelm II.

By the late nineteenth century, many Germans (including the Kaiser) regarded the Jews - never more than one per cent of the population - as a problem. While virulent racist anti-Semitism was growing in strength, there were still Germans who held traditional Christian anti-Semitic views and disliked Jews for being 'Christ killers'. Anti-Semitism may also have been encouraged by economic factors, especially the 'great depression' of the late nineteenth century. Those groups hit by economic and social change (peasant farmers, shopkeepers and skilled workers) were easily persuaded that Jewish financiers - who held a powerful position in both Germany and Austria-Hungary - were to blame. Indeed, Jews became a convenient scapegoat for virtually everything perceived to be wrong in 'modern' German society. But, while there was general agreement that there was a Jewish problem, there was no consensus about the solution. Some thought Jews ought to be fully assimilated. Others favoured re-introducing discrimination and forcing Jews to leave Germany. A few writers even talked in terms of annihilation. If the Jews were really the threat that racial anti-Semitic propaganda implied, if the difference between them and Aryans really was indelible and inscribed in the blood, then annihilation made logical - if perverse - sense. After all, expulsion meant merely a postponement of the problem and might lead to an increase of Jewish influence elsewhere in the world.

In the 1870s anti-Semitic parties formed and contested elections in both Germany and Austria. In Austria the Christian Social Party became a mass party on the strength of its anti-Semitic propaganda. In Germany, right-wing nationalist parties, which espoused anti-Jewish views, actually gained a majority in the Reichstag in 1893. Yet it is possible to exaggerate the strength of political anti-Semitism in Germany. The success of the nationalist parties in 1893 had relatively little to do with anti-Semitism. Indeed, no major German political party pre-1914 was dominated by anti-Semites and after 1900 the anti-Semitic parties were in steep decline, running out of voters and money. By 1912, the largest single party in the Reichstag was the Social Democratic Party, which was opposed to anti-Semitism. (Not unnaturally, it was supported by many German Jews.) Nevertheless by 1914, anti-Jewish feeling permeated broad sections of German society, and semi-political bodies and pressure groups (such as the Pan German League) which supported militant nationalism, imperial expansion and militarism, were strongly anti-Semitic. Ominously anti-Semitism was strongly entrenched within the academic community and teachers at every level were openly anti-Jewish.

However, before the First World War, anti-Semitism in Germany was no stronger than in many other countries. Indeed German Jews seemed in less danger than Jews in France or Russia. German Jews did not suffer extreme poverty, pogroms or legal discrimination. One reason for this was that power in Germany before 1918 was not invested in the people or in political parties. Instead, it lay with the Kaiser and in governments appointed by him. Although the Kaiser and many of his officials disliked Jews, they nevertheless felt a duty to protect them, believing, as the great German Chancellor Otto von Bismarck once put it, that the usefulness of the Jews was on the whole rather greater than the danger they presented.

4 Hitler and Anti-Semitism

a) Hitler's Early Views

Hitler, born in Austria in 1889, grew up in a society which was probably more anti-Semitic than Germany. A failed artist, Hitler did not move to Germany until 1913. Historians are divided about the extent to which he acquired his anti-Semitic views from his family and school, or from the years he spent in Vienna (1908-13). Hitler said that he first became anti-Semitic in Vienna. This is quite possible. Vienna contained large numbers of Jews and Hitler almost certainly read anti-Semitic newspapers and pamphlets. However, his own statements apart, there is no definite evidence that he was particularly anti-Semitic prior to 1914. In August 1914, with the outbreak of the First World War, Hitler volunteered to fight in the German army. Although never rising beyond the rank of corporal, he proved himself a brave soldier. Germany's defeat in November 1918 had a traumatic effect on him. Like many soldiers, he believed that the German army had been 'stabbed in the back' by the 'November criminals' - Marxists, socialists and Jews. Thereafter Hitler regarded Jews as a sinister enemy of Germany.

b) Psycho-historians and Hitler

Some (so-called) psycho-historians have tried to root Hitler's anti-Jewish obsession within his own psychology, paying particular attention to his childhood as a means of explaining his motivation and later behaviour. Most have claimed that Hitler's father was insensitive and domineering. His mother, by contrast, partly through a need to compensate for her 'guilt' at the deaths of her first three children, is usually seen as having an over-protective and unhealthy relationship with the infant Adolf. Supposedly this created feelings of extreme tension and insecurity in the young boy. Robert Waite, in his book *The Psychopathic God*, argued that Hitler's anti-Semitism arose from a dizzying array of neuroses and sub-conscious conflicts. Waite was even prepared to accept that Hitler may have believed in his own possible Jewish ancestry, seeing in this a powerful force pushing in the direction of genocide. Since he never knew whether one of his grandfathers was Jewish, Hitler had to prove to himself beyond a shadow of doubt that he could not possibly be corrupted by Jewish blood. Thus, according to Waite, he became history's greatest scourge of the Jews.

But it could be that Waite's views, and the views of other psycho-historians, have served only to muddy the waters. Labelling Hitler a 'neurotic psychopath'[4] or a 'borderline personality occupying the twilight zone between neurosis and psychosis'[5] does not help our understanding of the man. These labels, which mean different things to different psychiatrists, by themselves, tell us little about Hitler's mental state. Given that knowledge of Hitler's childhood is very limited, any serious investigation of his relationship with his mother and father is exceedingly difficult. Moreover, during his life he was not subject to any meaningful kind of psychological testing.

Unfortunately, too many psycho-historians have been far too selective in the evidence they have chosen to support a particular thesis.

c) Hitler's Views After 1918

There seems little doubt that the First World War had a dramatic effect on Hitler. Going into the war an aimless drifter, he came out a hard, resolute man with a sense of purpose. Germany's defeat may well have precipitated a severe personal crisis. It certainly seems to have been the reason why he turned his attention to politics. The fact that he was a veritable (if lowly) war hero gave him much-needed credibility in right-wing circles and undoubtedly helped his political career.

In September 1919 Hitler joined the small German Workers' Party, one of many similar *volkisch* groups which sprang up all over Germany after 1918. Within two years he was the leader (Führer) of the Party, now renamed the National Socialist German Workers' Party - or Nazi Party. By 1922 the Nazi Party was the largest right-wing party in Bavaria. In 1923 it was powerful enough to mount a serious attempt to overthrow the government, known as the the Beer Hall Putsch. This remarkable rise was the result of several factors. It was in part the triumph of Hitler's own will. Throwing himself into politics, he displayed oratorical, propagandist and organisational skills. But he was also helped by the chaotic conditions in Germany - especially Bavaria - in the years after 1918. Many Germans were looking for leaders who promised to re-establish Germany's greatness. Hitler promised that - and much more.

Hitler's views, which underpinned the aims of the Nazi Party, were by no means original. He simply rehashed Social Darwinist, nationalist and racist opinions that had circulated through Germany for several decades. But he did so in a way that gave the old ideas fresh impetus and ultimately far more significance. Hitler's ideology, which developed in Munich in the early 1920s (and which was probably influenced by right-wing intellectuals like Alfred Rosenberg and Dietrich Eckart), was presented to Germany and the world in a more fixed form in 1925 when the first volume of his book *Mein Kampf* was published. (It was written in Landsberg prison, where Hitler had been sent after the failure of the 1923 Putsch.)

Mein Kampf translates as 'My Struggle'. Struggle was the key word in Hitler's ideology.

1   The idea of struggle is as old as life itself for life is only preserved because other living things perish through struggle. ... In this struggle the stronger, the more able, win, while the less able, the weak, lose. Struggle is the father of all things. ... It is not by the principle of
5   humanity that man lives or is able to preserve himself above the animal world, but solely by means of the most brutal struggle. [6]

Hitler regarded the struggle between races as the central factor in the development of world history. In particular he saw a permanent struggle between the Aryan race and international Jewry. The Aryans were potentially the fittest people on earth, and upon their survival the existence of the planet depended. The Jews, on the other hand, were the ultimate adversary - 'parasites', 'leeches' and 'bloodsuckers' - who aimed to dominate the world themselves. Jews, in Hitler's view, constantly undermined a people's capacity for struggle, weakened and subverted its racial purity, poisoned its institutions and corrupted its positive qualities. Hitler held the Jews responsible for all Germany's misfortunes. He blamed them for defeat in war, for the Treaty of Versailles and for the establishment of the democratic (and weak) Weimar Republic. They were also responsible for a host of dangerous ideas - finance capitalism, internationalism, liberal democracy, and Marxism. Hitler particularly loathed Marxism (he made little distinction between communism and socialism) and saw Jews as the puppet masters of the USSR. (The fact that Jews were prominent in world and German communist and socialist movements lent some credence to his claim.)

There was more to Hitler's views than simple anti-Semitism. He believed that Nordic people headed the racial league table. All other peoples, particularly Slavs, Asiatics and Africans, were 'inferior'. The German people's duty was to increase in numbers in order to fulfil their destiny of world supremacy. To do this, they must remain racially pure: only pure-bloodedness assured a race's success. There was no room for pity or sentimentality in Hitler's ideology. His ideal government would be hard and ruthless, promoting the growth of the strongest and healthiest, not the weakest. A strong race would inevitably result in a strong nation. Hitler, an extreme nationalist, believed that Germany must struggle to gain its rightful place as the strongest nation on earth. To achieve this end, the Germans must win living space - *lebensraum* - at the expense of Poland and the USSR. Such a policy would ensure that the master-race Germans extended their power over inferior Slav peoples. Hitler had no time for democracy or for equality. If Germany was to achieve true greatness, the country must be ruled by the fittest individual who should be given absolute power. He envisaged a new social order in which class conflict and ideological divisions would disappear and be replaced by a sense of national solidarity: individuals would put the interests of the national community before their own selfish interests.

d) Conclusion

From the nightmare of Germany's defeat in November 1918, Hitler drew lifelong convictions. Anti-Semitism, in particular, became a central obsession. His anti-Semitic ideas were tirelessly reiterated and proclaimed. Germany must be prepared to take strong action to 'eliminate' the Jewish threat.

1 If just once at the beginning or during the course of the war we had
   exposed 12,000 or 15,000 of these Hebrew corrupters of the people to
   the poison gas that hundreds of thousands of our best German workers
   of every extraction and every profession had to endure at the front, the
5 sacrifice of millions of men would not have been in vain. On the
   contrary, if we had rid ourselves of those 12,000 or so fiends, we
   perhaps might have saved the lives of a million good, brave Germans.[7]

Hitler's ideas may not have been original but they were underpinned
by a simple (and terribly brutal) logic. Moreover, he was far from
being a cynical opportunist who adjusted his policies to circumstances
and who was bent on power simply for power's sake. Believing
passionately that he was on a mission of salvation for the German race
and nation, he maintained his views with remarkable consistency
from the 1920s until his death in April 1945. This fanatical conviction
was why he was ultimately such a danger.

5 Anti-Semitism in Germany: 1918-33

One of the main reasons for Hitler's rise to power was that large
numbers of Germans had some sympathy with his views. The fact that
Jews had played a prominent role in the left-wing revolutions in
Germany in the winter of 1918-19 helped encourage the view that
Jews were responsible for Germany's defeat. Many German nationalists also associated Jews with communism and believed that world
Jewry, with its headquarters in Moscow after the 1917 Russian revolution, was plotting to conquer Germany. In reality, the vast majority of
German Jews were not communists but moderate socialists or liberals
who supported the Weimar Republic. A few Jews became cabinet
members in the 1920s. (Perhaps the most famous was foreign minister
Walter Rathenau who was assassinated by extreme right-wing nationalists in June 1922.) However, this simply 'proved' to German nationalists that the hated Republic was indeed in Jewish hands. Germans
also identified Jews for their pernicious 'modern' influence on
German music, drama, film, art and architecture. Jewish financiers
were blamed for the severe depression which hit Germany after 1929.

   Most right-wing parties after 1918 were anti-Semitic. Virtually every
major German institution - the army, civil service, judiciary, churches
- was also permeated by anti-Semitism. Many Germans, young and old
alike, declared openly and proudly that they were anti-Semitic. Some
continued to believe in *The Protocols of the Elders of Zion*, which
purported to be a record of a secret meeting at which leading Jews
plotted world domination. *The Protocols* was exposed as a clumsy
Russian forgery as early as 1921, but many Germans continued to
accept the - implausible - idea of a joint conspiracy by Jewish international capitalists and Jewish Bolsheviks. It was easier to hold such views

than to accept the real and highly complex problems that faced Germany after 1918.

By the early 1930s the Nazis were the most enthusiastic exponents of anti-Semitism. It is hard to say how important this issue was for Nazi supporters. After all, anti-Semitic propaganda did not help Nazi popularity before 1930: in the 1928 elections the Nazis won less than three per cent of the total vote. Anti-Semitism in Germany in the early 1930s seems to have varied from place to place. Noakes' examination of Lower Saxony during the period 1930-3 suggests that most of the electorate were far more interested in economic matters than anti-Semitism. William Allen, after examining a single town in Lower Saxony, concluded that its residents 'were drawn to anti-Semitism because they were drawn to Nazism and not the other way round'.[8] Pridham, who has studied Bavaria, argues that Nazi activists were far more likely to hold aggressive anti-Semitic views than ordinary German voters. After reviewing the literature on several localities, Richard Hamilton concluded: 'If anti-Semitism was not a viable theme in a given area, it was played down or abandoned.'[9] However, Hamilton also believed that 'If it [anti-Semitism] was viable, it was given considerable play.'[10]

Certainly, the Nazis - and Hitler himself - adapted their message to the nature of the audience they were addressing. Hitler generally attacked Marxism as the main enemy in the early 1930s. But the claim that the Nazis toned down their anti-Semitic rhetoric as they made a serious bid for power has been accepted too readily. The fact was that Hitler and most leading Nazis believed that Jews and Marxists were basically synonymous. Attacks on Marxists, therefore, were essentially the same as attacks on Jews. In reality, Hitler held fast to his basic beliefs, not hiding the fact that he thought that behind every ill afflicting Germany, Jews were at work. It is doubtful whether most of those Germans who voted Nazi took seriously every Nazi anti-Semitic word and slogan. Nevertheless, most Germans certainly associated the Nazis with militant anti-Semitism.

By 1932 the Nazi Party had become the strongest political party in Germany. Germans voted Nazi for a variety of reasons. The world depression which caused high unemployment in Germany was a major factor. So was the fear of communism. Other Germans simply wanted strong government. After 1945 many of those who voted Nazi claimed that anti-Semitism was not the main reason why they had done so. But in the early 1930s, it does seem that large numbers of people of every class, age, region and gender, accepted the Nazi anti-Semitic message either fully or in part. Not all Germans who voted Nazi were vehemently anti-Semitic: few believed that Hitler would 'eliminate' all Germany's Jews. But most of the 44 per cent of Germans who voted Nazi in March 1933 expected - and many hoped - that Hitler would take some action against the Jews.

6 Hitler and the Nazi State

a) Hitler Comes to Power

On 30 January 1933, following a 'deal' with the leader of the conservative Nationalist Party, Hitler became Chancellor. He immediately called for new elections and in March 1933 the Nazis and their Nationalist allies (just) won an overall majority in the Reichstag. The Nazis immediately passed the Enabling Law which gave Hitler dictatorial powers. However, Hitler's powers were still not total. He could not ignore the views of the octogenarian President Hindenburg. Nor could he ignore those of conservative Nationalists in both his cabinet and the Army High Command. Hitler also had problems with his own SA (*Stürmabteilung*, or storm troopers) - the para-military wing of the Nazi Party. Many SA members (including the SA leader Ernst Röhm) wanted to implement radical Nazi policy immediately. Hitler, not wishing to alienate Hindenburg, the army and international opinion, determined to move cautiously.

In June 1934 Hitler had Röhm and other SA leaders arrested and shot. This 'Night of the Long Knives' helped Hitler win the support of the army. Following Hindenburg's death in August 1934, Hitler became effectively President and Chancellor. Henceforward, he was usually referred to simply as the Führer.

b) Hitler's Leadership Style

The spirit of the Third Reich (as Nazi Germany was now called) was embodied in Hitler's remark that there could be only one will in Germany, his own, and that all others had to be subservient to it. Importantly, Hitler had little interest in bureaucratic structures and the mentality which went with them. He saw politics essentially as the actions of great individuals and the solving of problems as a matter of will-power. Decision-making in the Third Reich was thus inspired by Hitler's personal whim rather than by administrative procedures. Increasingly he opted out of what he found to be the tedious routine of day-to-day government. Cabinet meetings became less frequent and were simply a sounding board for Hitler, who rejected the notion of reaching a collective decision through anything resembling a democratic process.

But the fact that Hitler was the Führer did not mean that he was able to initiate every major development in Germany. His power was restricted in several ways. Perhaps the main constraint was the sheer impossibility of one man keeping abreast of, let alone controlling, everything that was going on in Germany. Every day an enormous number of decisions had to be taken on a colossal range of issues. Hitler could not know about, even less decide upon, more than a tiny fraction of these matters. In consequence, it was not always clear exactly what his will was on any given matter. This problem was exacerbated by his leadership style. His preference for his home in Bavaria instead of Berlin, and his aversion to systematic work in general and paperwork in particular, meant that decision-making in Germany was often a chaotic process. Most of his involvement in government took the form of face-to-face encounters with subordinates, and decisions often took the form of a remark thrown out casually, which then became an 'Order of the Führer'. Little or no record often survives of these encounters. The process of Hitler's decision-making, therefore, confounds historians - just as it confounded civil servants at the time.

The problems did not end there. When there were - as often happened - competing views, Hitler sometimes found it difficult to make up his mind. There was some method in this. Often it was best to stand aloof and not interfere, hoping that matters would sort themselves out. But in any nation people tend to look to the head of government for instructions and decisions. This is even more true in a dictatorship. The fact that Hitler often declined to get involved in matters or took refuge behind open-ended generalities had a damaging effect on the smooth running of government.

Some 'functionalist' historians have argued that Hitler was a 'weak dictator' who took few decisions and who had difficulty getting those decisions implemented. In reality, Hitler was far from weak. He was ultimately the master in the Third Reich. Historians have often underestimated him. He did have some impressive qualities, including an excellent memory and a quick mind. He could work with discipline and tenacity in those areas which interested him. His will was not seriously challenged between 1934 and 1945: his decisions were put into practice. While he did not often involve himself in details of policy-making, he did reserve all fundamental decisions for himself.

c) Party Versus State

The Third Reich was not just a personal dictatorship. It was also a one-party state, in which the Nazi Party claimed sole political authority in every aspect of German life. Such totalitarian claims, augmented by a powerful propaganda machine, deceived many contemporaries into thinking that the Nazi state was an efficient and well-ordered system of government. The reality was different. This had much to do with the proliferation of bureaucracies and agencies in the Third Reich and the fact that there was no precise relationship between them. After 1933, state and Nazi Party institutions competed to implement a political programme which Hitler (both head of state and Party) often only outlined. Given that there was not much effort to regulate relations between Party and state, a complicated situation developed, often referred to as the 'dual state'. State civil servants for the most part were committed to legality and official procedures. Nazi activists, on the other hand, set on changing the world, were contemptuous of bureaucratic structures. Some wanted to smash the traditional elements of government in order to create a new Germany. Hitler, while having some sympathy with the Party radicals, recognised that the state bureaucracy was staffed by an educated and experienced personnel, and realised that its replacement by unqualified Party elements might well undermine his main goals. State and party agencies, therefore, functioned uneasily alongside each other at every level.

The situation was further complicated by the fact that the Nazi Party itself was by no means a unified whole. It consisted of a mass of specialist organisations - such as the Hitler Youth and the SA - keen to uphold their own particular interests. Hitler's tendency to create new agencies, usually headed by Party bigwigs, whose job was to speed up particular projects, added to the confusion. The situation was similarly - possibly more - confused in the regions. After 1933, in an attempt to replace the old federal structure, Germany was divided into 35 *Gaus* (or districts), each led by a *Gauleiter*. While *Gauleiters* were dedicated Party members, the Party, as such, had only tenuous control over them. *Gauleiters* regarded themselves as Hitler's personal agents, answerable only to him.

The fact that the Party lacked a unifying structure and had no central decision-making process reduced its influence. Indeed, the Party effectively disintegrated into its component parts with powerful Party leaders, like Goering and Himmler, building up their own autonomous empires and largely ignoring everyone, except Hitler.

d) 'Authoritarian Anarchy'?

Given that various power centres pursued their own particular interests without reference - indeed often in opposition - to others, it is easy to get the impression that 'the Third Reich was characterised by a degree of institutional anarchy that was unique - certainly in modern German history'.[11] Historians like Broszat and Mommsen have thus cast doubt on the extent to which the Nazi system was a product of conscious intention on Hitler's part. Mommsen has gone so far as to suggest that the anarchic system controlled Hitler, rather than he the system. In consequence, Broszat and Mommsen believe that historians should focus upon the structure of the Nazi state rather than upon Hitler himself. In this 'functionalist' view, many of the Nazi regime's measures, rather than being the result of long-term planning or even deliberate intent, were simply knee-jerk responses to the pressure of circumstance. Mommsen sees an improvised 'process of cumulative radicalisation', as subordinate organisations, vying with each other to maintain or acquire responsibilities, adopted the most radical of the available alternatives on the assumption that this reflected Hitler's will.

However, given that institutional conflict is endemic in virtually all government systems at all times, it may be that the functionalists have exaggerated the 'authoritarian anarchy' in the Third Reich. In reality, there was not always confrontation between the Party and state civil service. The bureaucrats in both camps often held similar views. Moreover, the men who staffed both the Party and state machinery conducted their business, for the most part, in line with tested German habits of order and obedience to authority. The special agencies Hitler set up were able to cut through red tape and get things done quickly. Nazi rule, therefore, was by no means always chaotic. Indeed, the idea of 'authoritarian anarchy' does not fit the remarkable successes of the Third Reich in various areas, not least the conquest of most of Europe. Finally, it should not be forgotten that Hitler retained the reins of power in his own hands. Sometimes he took a long time to make a decision but when he did his personal orders cut quickly through the administrative jungle. Most major aspects of Nazi policy - not least anti-Semitic action - were invariably in line with Hitler's conscious intentions.

7 The SS

Amidst all the confusion of state and Party structures there emerged a new and powerful organisation - the SS. Formed in 1925 as an elite bodyguard for Hitler, the SS remained a relatively minor section of the SA until Heinrich Himmler became its leader in 1929. Efficient and ambitious, Himmler envisaged the SS taking over the business of policing Germany and dealing with Germany's internal racial, ideological and moral enemies. In 1931 he created a special security service, the *Sicherheitsdienst* (SD), to act as the Party's own intelligence service. The SD had an aura of adventure and attracted young, well-educated Nazi idealists who were ready to carry out any order.

In the course of 1933-4, Himmler assumed control of all the political police in the German states, including the *Gestapo* (the secret state police) in Prussia. On 30 June 1934 Hitler turned to Himmler and the SS to carry out the purge of the SA. This purge greatly strengthened Himmler's position. The SS now became an independent organisation within the Party. By 1936 all police powers were unified under Himmler's control and he set about ensuring that both the *Gestapo* and the ordinary police drew closer to the SS. SS men were increasingly drafted into the police, and police officers were encouraged to join the SS. By 1939 Himmler had largely achieved his dream of creating an SS-Police.

Himmler thus became one of the key men in the Third Reich. By profession an agriculturist, he fervently believed in a biologically-oriented racism and was determined that the SS should become a racial elite, providing Germany with a new nobility. Himmler was more concerned about racial, physical and personal qualities (which he thought reflected race) than he was about education. Would-be SS recruits had therefore to go before a Racial Selection Board which imposed strict criteria for selection. Obsessed with racial purity, Himmler accepted only perfect Aryan specimens, preferably (but by no means only) tall, blond and blue-eyed. (Himmler himself hardly personified this perfect physical specimen!) Similarly, SS men were only allowed to marry women of 'good' German blood. Himmler was also concerned that the SS should have a strong consciousness of being the real core of the Nazi movement. He was keen, therefore, for the SS to adopt external marks of status, such as the striking black uniform. The SS made a fetish of honour, loyalty and unconditional obedience to Hitler. In November 1935, Himmler defined the goals of the SS as follows:

> 1 The first principle for us was and is the recognition of the values of blood and selection. ... The nature of the selection process was to concentrate on the choice of those who came physically closest to the ideal of Nordic man. External features such as size and a racially
> 5 appropriate appearance played and still play a role here ...
>   I know there are some people in Germany who feel sick at the sight of this black uniform; we can understand their feelings and do not expect many people to love us. All those who have the interests of Germany at heart will and should respect us, and those who somehow
> 10 some time have guilty consciences towards the Fuhrer or the nation should fear us. ... We shall unremittingly fulfil our task of being the guarantors of Germany's internal security, just as the German army guarantees the security of the honour, the greatness, and the peace of the Reich externally. We shall ensure that never again will the Jewish-
> 15 Bolshevist revolution of sub-humanity be unleashed in Germany, the heart of Europe, either from within or by emissaries from without.[12]

Himmler's right-hand man was Reinhard Heydrich, an ex-naval officer who became leader of the SD in 1931. Thereafter as Himmler rose, Heydrich rose with him. Tall, good-looking, a gifted athlete and highly intelligent, Heydrich was also totally ruthless. Hitler referred to him as the 'man with the iron heart'. The contemporary historian Burckhardt remarked that Heydrich was a 'young, evil god of death'.

8 Nazi Terror

In March 1933 Nazi activists, in the euphoria of victory, meted out vengeance on their political enemies. Leading socialists and communists were beaten up and herded into makeshift concentration camps where they were tortured and humiliated. These actions were largely spontaneous: they were not planned by Hitler. But Hitler saw nothing wrong with terror. 'Terror is the most effective instrument', he declared. 'I shall not permit myself to be robbed of it simply because a lot of stupid, bourgeois mollycoddlers choose to be offended by it.' In March 1933 Himmler established the first official concentration camp at Dachau. Soon other camps were brought under government supervision. By the summer of 1933 almost 30,000 people had been taken into 'protective custody' without trial and without the right of appeal.

Dachau became the model concentration camp. The camp commandant (from June 1933) was Theodor Eicke who imposed a system intended to rob the prisoners of their individuality and break their spirit. Shorn of their hair, prisoners were given a number - but no name. The camp guards - men of the SS Death Head units from 1936 - had total power and were trained in a way that was designed to destroy any feeling of humanity towards the inmates. Every conceivable - and some inconceivable - indignity was inflicted on the prisoners. Corporal punishment was routinely administered but it was also common for inmates to be urinated upon, to be thrown into cesspools, and to be hung from tree branches by the arms. The barely-fed prisoners were also expected to do hard physical labour.

By 1937 the three main camps - Dachau, Sachsenhausen and Buchenwald (see the map on page 26) - had only a few thousand prisoners. Some inmates had died. Others had been 'reformed' and released. However, the take-over of Austria and the Sudetenland in 1938 led to an increase in arrests. By September 1939 there were some 25,000 prisoners and three new camps - Flossenburg, Mauthausen and a woman's camp at Ravensbruck. People could be imprisoned for having a mentality hostile to the state. Even when individuals had been found innocent or had served their sentences, they could be re-arrested by the *Gestapo*/SD.

9 Nazi Propaganda

The Nazi regime did not maintain itself in power simply by the use of terror. From 1933 onwards, propaganda played a key role in winning over the hearts and minds of the German people to the ideas of National Socialism. The man most associated with propaganda was Joseph Goebbels, who became Minister of Popular Enlightenment and Propaganda in March 1933. Goebbels quickly brought all radio broadcasting under Nazi control and introduced various measures to achieve control of the press, cinema, theatre, literature and art.

Goebbels declared that no German in the Third Reich should feel himself to be a private citizen. The regime constantly urged people to work for the public good and to take part in Party activities. Efforts were made to create new kinds of social ritual. The *'Heil Hitler!'* greeting, the Nazi salute, and the militaristic uniforms were all intended to break down individuality and strengthen identification with the regime.

The mobilisation of youth was one of the most important goals of National Socialism. By 1939 the Hitler Youth Movement had nearly nine million members: it was virtually compulsory to belong to one of

The main concentration and extermination camps

its male or female organisations. The aim of the Hitler Youth was to ensure that young Germans were loyal to fatherland and Führer. Education was also used to indoctrinate. Ideologically unreliable teachers at all levels were dismissed and teachers' behaviour closely monitored. The aim of Nazi education was to ensure that German children were fit, disciplined and imbued with National Socialist ideas. Racial instruction became mandatory, although most teachers had little idea how to teach it at first and there were few materials or guidelines.

It is hard to say how effective Nazi propaganda was. The Nazis were well aware that they could not automatically mobilise public opinion. Indeed, the Party was keen to know the state of German opinion in order to be able to evaluate the popularity of its policies. Agencies were thus set up to try and track German opinion. The evidence from the surveys of these bodies suggests that Nazi rule was generally popular and Hitler far more popular than his party. The success of Nazi policies helped the propagandists. The Nazis did reduce unemployment. They did create a society in which most Germans felt they were working for the common good. There were also successes in foreign policy: re-armament (1935); the march into the Rhineland (1936); the take-over of Austria and then the Sudetenland (1938); and the annexation of part of the remainder of Czechoslovakia (1939). By 1939 Germany was again a major world power. Having seemingly redeemed Germany, Hitler became the focus of intense personal loyalty.

10 The Racial State

According to Nazi doctrine, a purified Aryan race, embodying all that was positive in humanity, was bound to triumph in the world struggle. Good 'blood', therefore, should be encouraged: people of 'inferior blood' - racial aliens and the mentally and physically handicapped - should be eliminated. The Nazis supported both eugenics (the desire to improve the stock of the nation) and euthanasia. Today euthanasia refers to the practice of so-called 'mercy killing' - painlessly ending the life of a person who is terminally ill at his/her request or, if the person is no longer capable of making such a request, then with the consent of relatives. It remains a controversial issue. Many Germans in the early-twentieth century believed that the criterion for mercy killing should not be the welfare - or even the wishes - of the individual patient but whether or not the individual was of value to the community. The concept of the destruction of worthless life was promoted by the publication of a book by Professor Binding and Professor Hoche in 1920, entitled *Permission for the Destruction of Worthless Life, its Extent and Form*. Binding and Hoche argued that Germany had become lumbered with 'living burdens' who were absorbing a disproportionate amount of national resources.

Hitler made his views clear in a speech at the Nuremberg Party rally in 1929:

1 If Germany was to get a million children a year and was to remove 700-800,000 of the weakest people then the final result might even be an increase in strength. The most dangerous thing is for us to cut off the natural process of selection. ... As a result of our modern sentimental
5 humanitarianism we are trying to maintain the weak at the expense of the healthy. It goes so far that a sense of charity, which calls itself socially responsible, is concerned to ensure that even cretins are able to procreate while more healthy people refrain from doing so. ... Degenerates are raised artificially and with difficulty. In this way we are
10 gradually breeding the weak and killing off the strong.[13]

After 1933 doctors, scientists and academics quickly adjusted to the new political realities. Joining hands with the government in a common struggle against 'degeneration', they offered courses on race and eugenics to teachers, nurses and civil servants and also helped by providing (apparently) precise definitions of groups and individuals who were perceived to be a danger to society.

In July 1933, the Nazis passed the Law for the Prevention of Offspring with Hereditary Diseases. This law, the cornerstone of the regime's eugenic legislation, permitted the compulsory sterilisation of anyone suffering from a hereditary disease and/or deemed to be mentally or physically unfit. These included anyone affected by congenital feeble-mindedness, schizophrenia, epilepsy, blindness, deafness, severe physical deformity, and severe alcoholism. The law did not apply to members of the Nazi Party. (Had it done so, Goebbels with his club foot, might have been forced to undergo a vasectomy.) While the handicapped could apply for sterilisation, applications could also be made by doctors or by directors of hospitals, homes and prisons. Some 220 hereditary health courts were set up, comprising a judge and two doctors. If these courts decided in favour of sterilisation, it was compulsory.

The law became operational in 1934 and had an immediate impact. The number of denunciations (mainly by doctors) was enormous - nearly 400,000 during 1934-5. Not all denunciations led to immediate decisions by the health courts, however. Only some 250,000 cases had been settled by 1937, mainly because the courts were overloaded. Of the cases settled, the vast majority - over 80 per cent - resulted in sterilisation. Initially the methods of sterilisation were vasectomies for men and tubal ligations for women. (Castration was authorised in November 1933 as a preventive punishment for sex offenders.) The primary victims of compulsory sterilisation were patients of hospitals and nursing homes. The majority were diagnosed as suffering from feeble-mindedness. This diagnosis was usually based on the results of a specially constructed intelligence test.

Sterilisation was by no means the only measure taken to protect the race. On the positive side, financial incentives (for example, increased family allowances) were given to encourage healthy parents to have more children - to produce the future 'national comrades'. German mothers who had large families were held in esteem and given an award - the Mothers' Cross: gold for those having eight children, silver for those with six and bronze for those with four. Attempts were also made to restrict access to contraceptive information and devices.

Little sympathy was shown to those considered to be racially, physically or mentally flawed. The Law for the Protection of the Hereditary Health of the German Nation (October 1935) prohibited a marriage if either party suffered from mental derangement or had a hereditary disease. Hitler was keen to go further and introduce a euthanasia programme. But he was aware that this was likely to arouse opposition, especially from the Catholic Church. In 1935 he told the Reich doctors' leader, Dr Wagner, that in the event of war he would take up the question of euthanasia. He believed that war would create the necessary conditions in which there would be limited opposition to such a step. Meanwhile, the Nazi government set about laying the groundwork for a euthanasia programme. In the late 1930s it mounted a massive propaganda campaign with horrific photographs of the insane prominently displayed in the popular press. There were also numerous articles on the intolerable cost of looking after psychiatric patients: the money, it was claimed, could be better spent on improving the lot of ordinary Germans. By 1939 the idea of euthanasia was being seriously canvassed among senior officials directly responsible for the mentally ill.

The Nazis also took action against the so-called 'asocial' - beggars, alcoholics, habitual criminals and homosexuals. Anyone who was labelled asocial could be taken into protective custody (i.e. sent to a concentration camp) and some were forcibly sterilised. The 30,000 German Gypsies were similarly targeted. Divided into two major groups, the Sinti and the Roma, Gypsies had long been unpopular in Germany and had often been persecuted. This persecution intensified after 1933. Although not mentioned specifically in the regime's major racial legislation, Gypsies were soon treated as second-class citizens. However, the Nazis had some difficulties in defining exactly who a Gypsy was. In 1936, Dr Robert Ritter became director of a research unit which had one task: to locate and classify all Germany's Gypsies. In the late 1930s thousands of Gypsies were concentrated in special camps.

11 Conclusion

Goebbels' propaganda gave the impression that Hitler was a far-seeing man of genius, brilliantly steering the German ship of state towards the goals of National Socialism. In reality, Hitler was not as exceptional as most Germans were led to believe. Nor was his government the efficient machine it was portrayed to be. However, to claim that Hitler was a weak dictator is to misconstrue the situation. In theory and in practice, Hitler's will in the Third Reich was law. He did not - and could not - concern himself with everything. However, in those areas he considered vital, Hitler did provide the lead. He took the strategic decisions; subordinates hammered out the details. Convinced that he was chosen by Providence to lead the Germans in their struggle for national existence, he did not lack firmness of purpose. Moreover, as far as we can tell, Hitler was popular with most Germans. After 1933, therefore, he was in a position to translate his ideology into reality. Essentially, he was determined to create a new racial and social order which would be strong enough to dominate first Europe and ultimately the world. Anti-Semitism was central to Hitler's ideology. Given his views, the position of the 500,000 Jews in Germany in 1933 was unlikely to be pleasant.

References

1   W. Shirer, *The Rise and Fall of the Third Reich* (Secker and Warburg, 1960), p. 43.
2   H. Graml, *Anti-Semitism in the Third Reich* (Blackwell, 1992), p. 57.
3   S. Friedländer, *Nazi Germany and the Jews: The Years of Persecution 1933-39* (Weidenfeld & Nicolson, 1997), p. 90.
4   See William Carr, *Hitler: A Study in Personality and Politics* (Edward Arnold, 1978), p. 149.
5   Ibid, p. 149.
6   D.Burrell (ed), *Nazi Germany Teaching Unit, Nazi Philosophy: General Views* (Longman, 1972), p. 7.
7   K.P. Fischer, *Nazi Germany: A New History* (Constable and Company, 1995), p. 169.
8   William S. Allen, *The Nazi Seizure of Power: The Experience of a Single German Town, 1930-1935* (Franklin Watts, 1973), p. 77.
9   Richard F. Hamilton, *Who Voted for Hitler?* (Princeton University Press, 1983), p. 606.
10 Ibid, p. 606.
11 J. Noakes and G. Pridham (eds), *Nazism 1919-1945: 2: State, Economy and Society 1933-1939* (University of Exeter, 1984), p. 204.
12 Ibid, p. 496.
13 Ibid, 3: *Foreign Policy, War and Racial Extermination* (1988), p.1002.

Source-based questions on 'Anti-Semitism and Nazism'

Read the extracts from Hitler on pages 16, 18 and 28 and that of Himmler on page 24. Answer the following questions:
a) What did Hitler mean by 'our modern sentimental humanitarianism' (page 28, lines 4-5)? (4 marks)
b) Comment on Himmler's phrase 'the Jewish Bolshevist revolution of sub-humanity' (line 14). (4 marks)

Summary Diagram
Anti-Semitism and Nazism

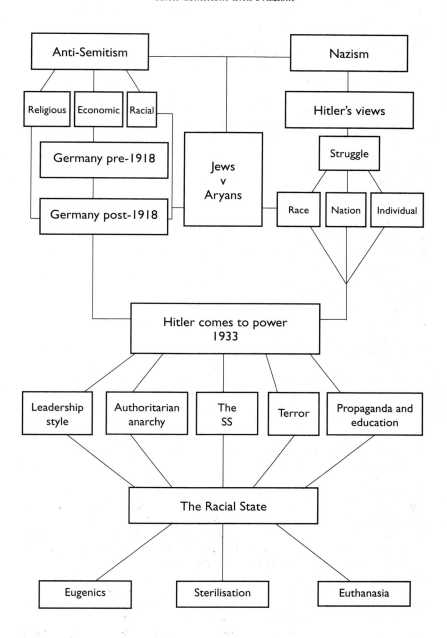

c) In what ways are the views presented in all four extracts consistent? (8 marks)

d) Why were the views expressed in the extracts a potential threat to German Jews? (5 marks)

e) Hitler expressed these views in the 1920s. Does this mean that he was likely to hold similar views in the 1930s? Explain your answer. (5 marks)

f) Why might Himmler's speech have appealed to SS men? (4 marks)

g) How might Hitler's views be challenged today? Would there have been similar challenges to Hitler's views in the 1920s and 1930s? (10 marks)

Hints and Advice

Source-based questions are now very much a part of virtually all history examinations, and therefore you must have practice at answering them. The first requirement is a clear understanding of the passages. So read them through slowly several times. The second requirement is to use your knowledge of the general context in order to help interpret the passages. In other words, bring your existing knowledge to bear. The third requirement is to answer the precise question set. Choose your words carefully, remembering that quality, not quantity, gets the best mark.

a) Consider what Hitler's main views were. Was he in favour of 'modern sentimental humanitarianism'? What kinds of views did he think Germans should have?

b) Treat this question as an opportunity to show that you are aware that Hitler, Himmler and many Nazis regarded Jews and communists (or Bolsheviks) as more or less one and the same. Why was this? Where was the supposed centre of the Jewish Bolshevist threat? What did Himmler mean by 'sub-humanity'?

c) At first reading, the four extracts may not appear to have much in common. They deal with a variety of Nazi concerns. However, in reality, the four extracts do have a great deal in common. Nazi views tend to be brutally consistent and coherent once you realise that the base line is 'struggle'. That should be a major clue to answering this question.

d) One of the sources is obviously a threat to Jews. But arguably all are a potential threat. Why?

e) This type of question should enable you to display your knowledge about Hitler's ideology. Politicians can - and often do - change their views. Was Hitler any different? Did he change his views?

f) This is perhaps the easiest question. Obviously Himmler is speaking to the converted. He is also spelling out the importance of the SS to the Nazi movement and to Germany.

g) This question allows you to be really creative! Most people today find Hitler's views abhorrent. Why? Many people in the 1920s and 1930s (including many Germans before 1933) also found Hitler's views abhorrent and for similar reasons as people today. However, more people in the 1920s and 1930s than today (and not only Germans) found some - if not all - of Hitler's views appealing. Why was this? Why are people more likely to be critical today than they were in the 1920s and 1930s?

3 Anti-Semitism in Action: 1933-9

1 Introduction

As far as Hitler and hard-core Nazis were concerned, anti-Semitism was an article of faith. Some action against the perceived Jewish arch-enemy was thus inevitable after 1933. While the Nazi Party had not prepared a detailed step-by-step programme of anti-Jewish measures which could immediately be implemented on coming to power, Hitler certainly had in mind the major lines of future action. These included the exclusion of Jews from public office, a ban on Jewish-German marriages, and efforts to 'persuade' Jews to emigrate. Nevertheless, Hitler soon found that translating his racist message into political action was far from simple.

In 1933 (and beyond) Nazi anti-Semitic policy was shaped by several factors. In the first months of power, Hitler could not ignore the views of President Hindenburg and his conservative allies who, while having little sympathy for the Jews, were less anti-Semitic than the Nazis. Hitler also realised that it might be necessary to play down extreme anti-Semitism in the interests of internal stability and economic progress. Nor could he ignore international opinion. Harsh measures against the Jews could lead to an international back-lash which could have serious foreign policy consequences. Germany's relatively weak position in international affairs in 1933 thus afforded Jews a degree of protection.

While Hitler had little interest in many aspects of domestic policy, most historians now accept that he determined the main strands of anti-Jewish policy. This is not to say that his hatred of the Jews was at all times the dominant strain in his political strategy. Between 1933 and 1939 he demonstrated that he knew how to tailor his anti-Semitic policies to fit the circumstances.

2 The Situation in 1933

In 1933 there were 503,000 Jews in Germany, comprising 0.76 per cent of the population. Of these 355,000 lived in cities of over 100,000 people. Most were reasonably prosperous, and many had their own businesses or held professional posts. sixteen per cent of Germany's lawyers, ten per cent of its doctors and five per cent of its newspaper editors were Jewish.

In the first months of 1933 SA units, in particular, took violent action against the Jews. This so-called 'revolution from below' was at its height in March 1933. Nazi mobs spread terror through the streets, beating up and sometimes killing individual Jews and sending hundreds to concentration camps. Jewish property was destroyed and some synagogues were burned down. The American consul in Leipzig reported on 5 April, 1933:

1   In Dresden ... uniformed 'Nazis' raided the Jewish Prayer House, inter-
    rupted the evening religious service, arrested twenty-five worshippers,
    and tore the holy insignia or emblems from their head-covering worn
    while praying. Eighteen Jewish shops, including a bakery, mostly in
5   Chemnitz, had their windows broken by rioters led by uniformed
    'Nazis'. Five of the Polish Jews arrested in Dresden were each compelled
    to drink one-half litre of castor oil. As most of the victims of assault are
    threatened with worse violence if they report the attacks, it is not
    known to what extent fanatical 'Nazis' are still terrorizing Jews,
10 Communists, and Social Democrats. ... Some of the Jewish men assaulted
    had to submit to the shearing of their beards, or to the clipping of their
    hair. ... One Polish Jew in Chemnitz had his hair torn out by the roots.[1]

The Nazi government tried to play down the incidents, claiming that
they were the work of 'popular anger'. The attacks were, indeed, initiated at local level by rank and file activists. Although sympathising
with the Nazi activists, Hitler realised that the attacks on Jews were in
danger of getting out of hand and threatened to endanger his
alliance with the conservative elite. He therefore appealed to his
followers to desist from violence. The attacks diminished - but did not
altogether cease.

    Such anti-Jewish violence led many Americans to call for a boycott
of German merchandise. Hitler, claiming that this anti-German
campaign was organised by Jews, decided to take retaliatory action.
On 1 April 1933, Goebbels, on Hitler's instructions, organised an official boycott against Jewish businesses throughout Germany. SA men
enforced the boycott by standing in front of thousands of Jewish
shops and businesses. Yet this boycott proved generally ineffective.
Problems arose over defining exactly what was and what was not a
Jewish shop or firm. (Many 'Jewish' firms were controlled by foreign
creditors or by German banks or were half-Jewish and half-German.)
Some Germans insisted on shopping in Jewish shops to demonstrate
their disapproval of Nazi policy. International protests and the likely
effects of further retaliation resulted in Hitler calling off the boycott
after only one day. (It had originally been intended to go on indefi-
nitely.) He had no wish to damage the still precarious German
economy. However, at the local level some Nazi activists continued the
boycott - with varying success - and the situation remained confused
for many months. While most local authorities turned a blind eye, a
few upheld the law and occasionally arrested SA men for preventing
Germans from entering Jewish shops.

    Hitler, while officially opposing violence, supported formal anti-
Semitic legislation. From April 1933 there was a flood of laws, aimed at
depriving Jews of their rights and livelihoods. Perhaps the most important of these was the Law of the Restoration of the Professional Civil
Service (7 April 1933). This introduced 'Aryanism' as a prerequisite

for holding civil service positions, thus automatically excluding Jews from such positions. However, none of the Party research institutes, set up to investigate Jewish matters, ever succeeded in pinpointing a particular Jewish blood type, physical characteristic or other biological evidence of race. The Law was thus forced to use religion, not racial criteria, as a defining characteristic. According to the Law, 'Anyone who is descended from non-Aryan parents or grandparents, and particularly from Jews, counts as non-Aryan. It is sufficient if one parent or grandparent is not Aryan.' Similar laws aimed at excluding Jews from other professions, including the legal profession, were passed in rapid succession.

While most Germans seem to have welcomed such laws, some believed that Jews who had loyally served Germany should be differentiated from those who had not. Hindenburg took a stand on this issue by demanding the inclusion of an exemption clause for those who had fought - or whose fathers or sons had been killed - during the First World War. In a letter to Hitler in April 1933, Hindenburg said he thought discrimination against Jews who 'were good enough to fight and give their blood for Germany' was 'quite intolerable'.[2] Hitler, possibly underestimating the number of Jews who would thus be exempted, assured the President that he would endeavour to do 'all possible justice' to these 'noble sentiments'.[3] As a result, over 60 per cent of 'non-Aryan' lawyers, for example, retained the right to practise. However, the government immediately set about circumventing the conditions of exemption by introducing ever more stringent conditions into the relevant paragraphs of the laws.

Anti-Semitic measures were also introduced in a host of other areas. A law against the overcrowding of schools (April 1933) severely limited Jewish enrolment in public schools. University places for Jewish students were also restricted. In late September and early October 1933 Jews were banned from joining the mandatory guilds for employees in the fields of film, theatre, music, fine arts and journalism. Anti-Semitic measures were also initiated by local authorities and by professional organisations.

Nazi policy, it should be said, was not particularly well-planned or well co-ordinated at this time. At a cabinet meeting on 7 April 1933, Hitler specifically excluded Jewish doctors from the application of the Aryan clause; but his wishes were ignored by Nazi local authorities, which proceeded to ban Jewish doctors on their own initiative. Consequently, on 22 April, the Reich government, in the interests of consistency, issued a regulation banning Jewish doctors. The pace at which Hitler's government moved, therefore, was partly effected by grass roots pressure (as well as pragmatism).

In 1933, most Jews, including many who had long since forgotten that there was any connection between themselves and the Jewish community, found life in Germany increasingly difficult. As well as enduring discriminatory legislation, they also faced the persistent anti-

Semitic rabble-rousing of the Nazi press, especially Julius Streicher's *Der Stürmer* newspaper. After 1933 this paper acquired a semi-official character and sold widely, pouring out scurrilous and pornographic attacks on the Jews. (Even some hardened Nazis found Streicher's material objectionable.) Ordinary Germans were deterred from cultivating personal contacts with Jews. Indeed, there was growing animosity at every level of society. Jewish children at mixed schools were humiliated. Jewish students - and academics - were driven from universities. Jews found themselves excluded from clubs and associations. There was also considerable pressure on them to close down their businesses or sell them - at bargain prices. While the majority of those involved in anti-Jewish activity were Party members, most Germans seemed to approve of the discriminatory measures. Even Church leaders did not speak out against Nazi actions. When they did speak at all about anti-Semitism, they were most likely to speak in support of the Nazis rather than against the Jewish persecution.

3 1934: A Year of Calm?

In 1934 the Nazis put anti-Semitic legislation on the back-burner. Once Hjalmar Schacht became Minister of Economics in 1934, noninterference with Jewish business was quasi-officially agreed upon. Jewish firms were making too important a contribution to the German economy to be sacrificed on the altar of popular anti-Semitism. Across the country, people, unwilling to forego the services of Jews (especially as shopkeepers and market dealers), continued to do business with them. For the time being, economic realism triumphed over ideological prejudice.

But action from 'below' did not stop. Many restaurants and hotels, sometimes whole villages, had signs: 'Jews not wanted here'. Individual Jews were often humiliated by members of the SA or Hitler Youth. Jewish economic survival became increasingly difficult, especially in rural areas. By making their lives difficult, the Nazis hoped to encourage Jews to emigrate. However, many Jews, especially the older ones who had lived all their lives in Germany, were reluctant to leave. Most hoped that the persecution was a passing phase. Those who did wish to emigrate also faced difficulties. Barred from taking most of their assets out of Germany, they soon discovered that countries like Britain, USA and France, themselves suffering from high unemployment, were reluctant to take in large numbers of impoverished Jews. Moreover German Jews had to compete with hundreds of thousands of Jews fleeing from other anti-Semitic states in eastern Europe.

Some 37,000 Jews left Germany in 1933. They included some prominent people - not least Albert Einstein, who described what was happening in Germany as a 'psychic illness of the masses'.[4] But in 1934 departures diminished to 23,000. German Jews were by no means united on how to respond to the Nazis. Most Jewish organisations encouraged Jews to keep their heads down, hoping the crisis would blow over. Reckoning that the responsibilities of power, the influence of conservative members of the government and a watchful outside world would exercise a moderating influence on any Nazi tendency to excess, they also believed that good behaviour on their part might encourage tolerance on the part of the Nazis. But Jewish hopes of appeasing the Nazis - who were opposed to any idea of assimilation - were still-born. Instead, Nazi agencies encouraged the Jews to see themselves as having a separate identity and generally supported the idea of Zionism - that Jews should be given their own homeland in Palestine (then under British control). Zionist organisations in Germany, therefore, received preferential treatment. Rich Jews were also permitted to move a large part of their possessions to Palestine, in exchange for agreeing to facilitate an increase in German exports. Indeed, some Zionists supported Nazi policies on the grounds that large-scale Jewish emigration from Germany would encourage the development of Palestine. Britain, however, was reluctant to allow more Jewish settlers into Palestine because of opposition from native Palestinians.

4 The Nuremberg Laws

Even before coming to power, the Nazis had been keen on stopping marriages - and sexual relations - between Jews and Germans. Although there was a great deal of discussion on this matter after 1933, little was immediately done. There were several problems. First there was opposition from those like Schacht who feared the possible international consequences of racist measures. Secondly the government was still unable to agree definite criteria for establishing an individual's race. The result was that nothing emerged from various ministerial departments except draft legislative proposals. In the spring of 1935 there was pressure from influential men like Streicher and Goebbels to do more. Nazi newspapers published a host of lewd stories which implied that thousands of German girls were being raped by Jews. From May to August 1935 local Party organisations, disappointed at what they saw as the regime's moderation, stepped up their actions against Jews. In many places the conditions which had prevailed in 1933 returned. There were renewed attacks on synagogues and Jewish shops. While Hitler may well have sympathised with the grass roots anti-Jewish campaign, he distanced himself from developments. Indeed in August, having seemingly decided that the 'terror' posed dangers to German trade, he spoke out against unauthorised actions and the anti-Semitic campaign quietened down.

But demands for a 'Blood Protection Law' which would prevent marriages between Jews and Germans continued to grow. In July 1935 Minister of the Interior Frick instructed registrars to stop performing 'racially mixed marriages' and indicated that the government intended to regulate the question of such marriages by law in the very near future. However, by September legislation had still not appeared. Hitler was to 'remedy' this situation at the Nuremberg Party rally which took place in mid-September 1935.

Some historians think that Hitler had not initially planned to use the occasion of the Nuremberg rally to introduce legislation to regularise the question of mixed marriages and Jewish citizenship. They claim that Hitler summoned the Reichstag and diplomatic corps to Nuremberg in order to make an important declaration on foreign, not anti-Semitic, policy. But, at the last minute, Hitler decided that the situation was not right to do so. Needing something important to say to fill the foreign policy gap, and encouraged by the atmosphere created by the mass of the Party's rank and file, he seized on the Jewish question. Accordingly, the argument goes, he abruptly summoned a variety of anti-Semitic experts to Nuremberg and asked them to draft a citizenship law and a law on mixed marriages. In the night-long deliberations that followed, four proposals, varying between a 'soft' Ministry and 'hard' Party line, were eventually drafted. Hitler then vacillated over which policy to adopt.

This version of events, it should be said, is based largely on the dubious evidence of one civil servant, on trial for war crimes after 1945, whose account was part of his defence. More plausibly, the laws which emerged in Nuremberg in 1935, rather than being improvised, were more the result of long-term planning. Certainly the issues underpinning the Nuremberg Laws had been long discussed, even if no agreement had been reached. It seems likely that Hitler had come to Nuremberg disgruntled at the failure of the bureaucrats to introduce legislation. Most people 'in the know' - ministers, civil servants, journalists, and leading Jews - expected legislation. The Party rally provided an appropriate occasion to unveil new measures which might satisfy Nazi radicals. Hitler can thus be seen as deliberately 'bouncing' the bureaucracy into producing the desired legislation.

Interestingly, Hitler decided to accept the two most moderate of the four draft laws. Introducing the new laws at Nuremberg, he spoke of them as a solution which 'perhaps' would lay the foundations for peaceful co-existence between Jews and Germans. But if the laws proved unsatisfactory, he would ask the Party to come up with a 'final solution'.

The Law for the Protection of German Blood and German Honour dealt with the situation regarding mixed marriages. Stating that 'the purity of German blood is essential to the further existence of the German people', the Law prohibited marriage and sexual relations between Jews and Germans. It also forbade Jews to display the national flag and prohibited Jews from employing German females under the age of 45 as domestic servants. The penalties for violating the Law ranged from fines and imprisonment to hard labour. Although the Law was seen as odious outside Germany, within

Germany it was not seen as particularly draconian. The ban on mixed marriages was already effectively in operation. Nor did the Law say that all existing mixed marriages were to be automatically dissolved.

The Reich Citizenship Law distinguished between citizens and subjects. Germans and people of kindred blood were to be fully-fledged citizens with full political rights. Non-Germans, on the other hand, were to be subjects, enjoying protection rather than political rights. Most Jews were initially relieved by this classification. The loss of Reich citizenship did not mean very much: the loss of the right to vote, for example, meant nothing in Nazi Germany. However, the fact remained that Jews were now officially second-class (non-)citizens. Moreover, the vagueness of the law played into Nazi hands by enabling Jewish rights to be stripped away piecemeal in a series of supplementary decrees over the following years.

The Nuremberg Laws symbolised the exclusion of Jews from the German national community. But the question of defining just who was Jewish - and thus who the Laws applied to - remained a major problem. The issue was discussed by racial and legal experts in the weeks after September 1935. Ministry of Interior officials, anxious to limit the number of people classified as Jews, pressed for half-Jews being accepted as Reich citizens. Nazi militants, on the other hand, thought that anyone who was only one-eighth Jewish should be classi-fied as a Jew. Hitler did not involve himself in this tortuous debate and avoided taking sides. His evasion tactics worked. In the end Party and Ministry experts managed to reach a compromise and on 14 November 1935 the First Supplementary Decree on the Reich Citizenship Law was enacted. A 'full Jew' was defined as someone who had three Jewish grandparents or someone who had two Jewish grandparents and who was married to a Jew. Those who had smaller fractions of Jewishness were labelled *Mischlinge* (half-breeds). *Mischlinge* were divided into half-breeds first degree (those with two Jewish grandparents) and second degree (those with one Jewish grandparent). *Mischlinge* second degree were essentially regarded as Aryans and did not face much discrimination, unless they belonged to a Jewish religious community or were married to a Jew. *Mischlinge* first degree were, for the time being at least, allowed to attend both senior schools and universities: they were also eligible for military service. Nevertheless they did face some discrimination. While marriages between *Mischlinge* first degree and Aryans (or *Mischlinge* second degree!) were permissible by special dispensation, such dispensations were rarely given. *Mischlinge* first degree, therefore, were effectively forced to marry into the Jewish community. They were also barred from certain professions. However, by providing a narrow definition of 'Jewishness', the Decree excluded some 250,000 half-Jews from much of the anti-Jewish legislation which followed. *Mischlinge* first degree remained relatively safe in Nazi Germany.

The Citizenship Laws proved to be a nightmare to interpret. The exact determination of who was a Jew often involved scores of 'family researchers' hunting down the necessary birth certificates or other legal documents to establish people's racial purity. There were large numbers of special cases (which later became a matter of life and death). Ironically the Nazi regime, which prided itself on the scientific basis of its racism, was in the end obliged to fall back on a religious definition of race.

The Nuremberg Laws (including the Citizenship Law) were presented to radicals as a move to implement the Party platform. They were presented to conservatives as measures designed to ensure stability. They certainly seem to have been approved by most Germans, who accepted the idea of segregating Jews. Many hoped that by clarifying the status of Jews in Germany, the Laws would put an end to disorder and violence. Hitler, still concerned with the international ramifications of anti-Semitic policy, had been prepared to compromise between the moderate civil servants and Nazi radicals. The historian Phillipe Burrin thinks his behaviour in the autumn of 1935 was characteristic: 'He had developed a technique of postponing decisions until, after lengthy discussions, the parties were ready to welcome his intervention with relief. In this case ... he had, through his temporizing tactics, induced his lieutenants to accept a point of view more moderate than their own'.[5]

5 The Calm Before the Storm: 1936-7

In 1936 Germany staged the winter and summer Olympic Games. Hitler's government, anxious to make the Games a success and concerned that overt anti-Semitism might induce several countries to withdraw their teams, adopted a more moderate line. The murder of a Nazi official by a Jew in Switzerland in February 1936, just as the winter Olympics were about to begin, was thus played down. The period of relative calm extended over the summer and many Jews hoped that the Nuremberg Laws were indeed the 'final solution'. There was thus no great sense of urgency about emigration: indeed, some of the 75,000 Jews who had fled Germany in the years 1933-5 now returned.

However, the harassment of Jews did not altogether cease. Decrees on implementing the Nuremberg Laws continued to be issued and dozens more occupations were forbidden to Jews. Streicher and other militant anti-Semites continued to demand more radical measures. At the 1936 Party conference Streicher asserted that the Nazis 'had declared a war on the Jews which [would] end in their annihilation'. German propaganda continued to convey a negative image of the Jew. In particular, Goebbels tried to build on the impression of Jews as foreigners by creating in people's minds a stereotype of the ghetto Jews of eastern Europe - far from the reality of the assimilated German Jew. See, for instance, the Nazi poster for the film *The Eternal Jew*.

Nazi poster from the 'Eternal Jew' exhibition, 1937

(Note the Jew's garb, beard and sidelocks: note also what he is carrying.) The impact of Nazi propaganda, however, can be exaggerated. It probably did little more than reinforce existing negative images of Jews.

By 1937 the SS was increasingly asserting its claim to a major role in the formation of Jewish policy. Leading SS officials were not interested in the crude, bully-boy tactics of the SA: they were more concerned with establishing clear criteria and professional systems which would enable them to find a final solution to the Jewish question. In autumn 1936 the SD established a separate section for Jewish affairs: its deputy head was Adolf Eichmann, an Austrian who had already established a reputation for himself as an 'expert' on Jewish matters. As an important first step, the section set about gathering detailed information about individual Jews and Jewish organisations. Its ideal solution to the Jewish question was mass emigration. But serious obstacles in the way of emigration continued.

The fact that one office of the SD tried to encourage Jews to emigrate, while other agencies complicated that process by stripping them of their capital, was indicative of the confusion that reigned in this and other spheres of Jewish policy. Hitler intervened only occasionally, sometimes to insist that economic matters should have priority, but at other times to affirm a hard anti-Semitic line in relation to some particular measure that was in dispute. In April 1937 Hitler explained his somewhat cryptic position to Party leaders. After emphasising that the final aim of Nazi Jewish policy was 'crystal clear to all of us', he added:

1   All that concerns me is never to take a step that I might later have to retrace and never to take a step which could damage us in any way. You must understand that I always go as far as I dare and never further. It is vital to have a sixth sense which tells you broadly what you can and
5   cannot do. Even in a struggle with an adversary it is not my way to issue a direct challenge to a trial of strength. I do not say, 'Come and fight me because I want a fight'; instead I shout at him, and I shout louder and louder, 'I mean to destroy you'. Then I use my intelligence to help me to manoeuvre him into a tight corner so that he cannot strike back, and
10 then I deliver the fatal blow.[6]

6 Increasing Pressure: 1937-8

By the end of 1937 Germany was re-arming and its economic position was stronger. Hitler, therefore, had less reason to fear international response to anti-Semitic measures. In November 1937 he decided he could afford to dismiss Schacht from his post as Minister of Economics. Schacht was the first victim of a major purge of conservatives in the administration, army, and diplomatic corps during the winter of 1937-8. This purge ended the delicate balance between the

Nazis and the traditional elites which had lasted since 1933. This was bad news for Jews because the conservatives had been a major barrier to radical anti-Semitism.

Goering now took over Schacht's responsibilities, integrating the Economics Ministry into his Four Year Plan organisation. Given that one of Goering's secret objectives was to prepare the German economy for war, the Jewish issue took on a new dimension. There was suddenly increased pressure on Jewish businesses to 'voluntarily' sell out at a price well below the market value to German firms eager to benefit from the process of 'Aryanisation'. This process was encouraged by a number of decrees issued by Goering. Perhaps the most important was the Decree for the Registration of Jewish Property (April 1938), which declared that all Jews with property worth more than 5,000 marks had to register with the government. This decree was clearly intended as a preliminary move to pave the way for the confiscation of all Jewish property. Other decrees simply shut down a wide variety of Jewish shops, businesses and services. A law of July 1938, for example, excluded Jews from specified commercial occupations. This resulted in the dismissal of some 30,000 Jewish travelling salesmen. Jews were also banned from employment as security guards, estate agents and travel agents. Of the 40,000 businesses still owned by Jews in April 1938, only about 20 per cent eluded liquidation or 'Aryanisation' over the next 12 months.

The aim of the discriminatory measures was to 'encourage' Jews to leave Germany. Indeed at the start of 1938 Hitler formally declared that he favoured encouraging emigration 'by every possible means'. Party radicals mounted yet another vigorous anti-Semitic campaign. Goebbels was particularly active in Berlin. Hundreds of Jews with police records (including those who only had parking fines) were rounded up and transported to concentration camps. Those who agreed to leave the country secured their release. In July 1938, the Interior Ministry, as part of the process of facilitating identification of Jews, decreed that (from January 1939) all male Jews must assume an additional first name of 'Israel', while all female Jews had to take the name of 'Sarah'.

This hardening of anti-Semitic activity was associated with - and possibly accelerated by - the Nazi take-over of Austria (the *Anschluss*) in March 1938. Austrian Nazis welcomed union with Germany and in the euphoria accompanying the *Anschluss,* there was a wave of spontaneous violence against Austria's 190,000 Jews. Many were beaten up and forced to wash streets, pavements and buildings in front of jeering crowds; others had their homes and businesses looted. Meanwhile the application of every sort of pressure forced many Jews to sell their businesses and possessions at rock bottom prices. By mid-May 1938 a Property Transfer Office, with 500 employees, was busy promoting the Aryanisation of Jewish economic assets. By the end of the year over half the houses and flats owned by Jews in Vienna had been Aryanised.

Austria also became a kind of laboratory for SS emigration policy. In August 1938 Eichmann set up in Vienna a Central Office for Jewish Emigration, concentrating all the various service personnel specialising in emigration matters in one building. Eichmann's methods allowed an applicant to complete in one day procedures which in Germany required many weeks. Jews walked out of the Office with an emigration visa and little else. Virtually all their property was confiscated. By November 1938 Eichmann could claim to have overseen the forced emigration of 50,000 Austrian Jews (as opposed to 19,000 in Germany in the same period). By running roughshod over normal emigration procedures, he developed a programme of forced deportation that did not even guarantee acceptance at the other end. This ultimately led to well publicised international incidents of ships carrying Jewish refugees shuttling from port to port seeking permission to land their human cargo.

Harsh measures were taken against other 'foreign' Jews. In October 1938 Jews in the Sudetenland (just annexed by Germany) were deported to what remained of Czechoslovakia. The Czech government refused to accept them, even though, the previous month, they had been Czech nationals. After wandering in no man's land for several weeks, the Sudeten Jews were eventually taken in by various other countries. In 1938 the Polish government, itself strongly anti-Semitic, threatened to revoke the citizenship of Polish Jews living in Germany. The aim - to prevent Germany from sending these residents back to Poland - backfired. In October 1938 Hitler ordered the Polish Jews to be expelled to Poland. German police rounded up some 17,000 and dumped them at the Polish border in a state of utter destitution. The Polish authorities at first refused to accept them. Only after lengthy negotiations was a compromise agreement reached, by which Germany succeeded in getting rid of most of its 'undesirables'.

7 *Kristallnacht*

On 7 November 1938 Ernst von Rath, a German embassy official in Paris was shot (and mortally wounded) by a 17-year-old Polish Jew in response to the mistreatment of his parents and the thousands of other Polish Jews in Germany. Goebbels, hoping to get back into Hitler's good graces after a scandalous affair with a Czech film star, ensured that the German press waxed indignant over the shooting. This nationwide press campaign helped stir up trouble and on 8-9 November Jewish homes, businesses and synagogues were attacked by gangs of Nazis, acting largely on their own initiative and without specific instructions from above.

Interestingly, Hitler made no mention of the Paris shooting in his annual speech at the Burgerbraukeller in Munich on 8 November. The next day, however, Rath died of his wounds. News of his death reached Hitler at around 9 p.m. during the traditional 'Old Fighters' dinner held in the Munich town hall to commemorate the 1923 Putsch. An intense conversation immediately took place between Hitler and Goebbels, who was seated next to him. Hitler left soon after, without giving his usual speech. Goebbels spoke instead, delivering a bitter attack on the Jews and calling for Rath's death to be avenged. Making it clear that Hitler would not oppose 'spontaneous demonstrations' of the type that had already occurred, he left senior Nazis in no doubt about what was expected of them. After Goebbels had finished speaking, Party leaders immediately set about giving instructions via telephone and telegram to their subordinate organisations. Himmler was not present to hear Goebbels' speech with the result that the SS was not greatly involved in the operation which followed.

The violence on 9-10 November (*Kristallnacht* or the 'Night of Broken Glass'), orchestrated by Party activists (especially the SA), was much greater than the previous night. In some places, Nazi members acted alone. But elsewhere, ordinary Germans joined in the pogrom and the looting which accompanied it. Overnight close to 8,000 Jewish businesses were destroyed, 200 synagogues burned, hundreds of Jews beaten up and over 90 killed. Neither the fire brigade nor the police intervened to prevent the violence and destruction. That night and over the next few days some 30,000 Jewish men were herded into concentration camps. Most were later released but only in exchange for written promises to leave Germany.

On 21 November, the American consul in Leipzig prepared a detailed statement on the events. This is part of his report:

1 The shattering of shop windows, looting of stores and dwellings of Jews which began in the early hours of 10 November 1938, was hailed subsequently in the Nazi press as a 'spontaneous wave of righteous indignation throughout Germany'. ... So far as a very high percentage of the
5 German populace is concerned, a state of popular indignation that would spontaneously lead to such excesses can be considered as nonexistent. On the contrary ... all of the local crowds observed were furiously benumbed over what had happened and aghast over the unprecedented fury of Nazi acts that had been or were taking place
10 with bewildering rapidity throughout their city...

    At 3 a.m. on 10 November 1938 was unleashed a barrage of Nazi ferocity as had had no equal hitherto in Germany, or very likely anywhere else in the world since savagery began. Jewish buildings were smashed into and contents demolished or looted. In one of the Jewish sections an
15 18-year-old boy was hurled from a three-storey window to land with both legs broken on a street littered with burning beds and other household furniture and effects from his family's and other apartments. This information was supplied by an attending physician ...Although apparently centred in poorer districts, the raid was not confined to the humbler
20 classes. One apartment of exceptionally refined occupants ... was violently ransacked, presumably in search for valuables...

According to reliable testimony, the debacle was executed by SS men and Stormtroopers not in uniform, each group having been provided with hammers, axes, crossbars and incendiary bombs.[7]

Hitler seems to have been surprised by the extent of the pogrom. Goering, like many Germans, was horrified by the damage to property and worried about the potential economic effects. Himmler was highly critical of the undisciplined behaviour of the SA. A British official in Berlin claimed that he had not met 'a single German from any walk of life who does not disapprove to some degree of what has occurred'.[8] Not surprisingly, international opinion strongly condemned the violence. Goebbels' claim that *Kristallnacht* was a 'spontaneous' demonstration was dismissed as a crude lie. *The Times* spoke for most foreign opinion when it referred to the pogrom as 'an act of the Reich government'. [9]

But few ordinary Germans spoke out against *Kristallnacht*. No doubt this was partly because it was increasingly dangerous to do so. But there is plenty of evidence to suggest that large numbers of Germans were not opposed to the maltreatment of Jews. (Even leading Catholic and Protestant bishops did not condemn *Kristallnacht*.) Moreover, *Kristallnacht* had indicated that some Germans were delighted to kill Jews.

On 12 November Goering chaired an important inter-ministerial meeting to determine the implications of *Kristallnacht* and to plan future Jewish policy. Goebbels, Heydrich, economic, finance and foreign ministry officials, and insurance companies' representatives, were present. Goering began as follows:

1   Gentlemen! Today's meeting is of a decisive character. I have received a
    letter written on the Führer's orders ... requesting that the Jewish ques-
    tion be now, once and for all, co-ordinated and solved one way or
    another. And yesterday once again the Führer requested me on the
5   phone to take co-ordinated action in the matter ...
        I would not wish there to remain any doubt, gentlemen, as to the
    purpose of today's meeting. We have not come together simply for more
    talk but to make decisions, and I implore the competent agencies to take
    all measures to eliminate the Jew from the German economy and to
10 submit the measures to me, so far as it is necessary.[10]

A number of important actions followed this meeting. Blaming the Jews for *Kristallnacht*, the government seized the money the insurance companies were paying out for the damage inflicted on Jewish property. In addition, the Jewish community was forced to pay a collective fine of 1,000 million marks as compensation for the murder of Rath. (Needless to say, no German was ever prosecuted for arson, destruction of property or murder.)

Perhaps the most decisive measure taken on 12 November was the Decree Excluding Jews from German Economic Life. This formalised the extensive 'Aryanisation' of Jewish-owned property which had begun in the autumn of 1937. Goering announced that from 1 January 1939, all Jews were forbidden to undertake any form of independent business activity, from wholesale trade to corner shops. This law, plus a number of supplementary decrees, brought to an end any type of professional activity on the part of Jews which required contact with the Aryan world.

The 12 November meeting did not just concern itself with the economic situation. Goebbels demanded that Jews and Germans should be segregated in every sphere of life. Some two weeks later Himmler issued a tough police decree effectively banning Jews from visiting theatres, cinemas, concerts, exhibitions, cabarets and circuses. Hitler rejected the most radical proposals: Jews did not yet have to wear a distinctive badge and they were still to have access to public transport. However, over the winter of 1938-9, laws against Jews kept on appearing. The last Jews were driven from German schools and universities. Jews were forced to hand over their driving licences. They were not allowed to use sports grounds or public swimming baths. They were even prohibited from keeping homing pigeons!

Goering officially confirmed his claim to sole competence for the Jewish question in a letter to all government departments in December 1938. His authority, however, was being increasingly challenged by the SS, particularly as a result of a new emigration initiative, which resulted in part from *Kristallnacht.*

8 Emigration: 1938-9

In January 1939 Goering commissioned Heydrich to bring the 'Jewish question to as favourable a solution as present circumstances permit'. The solution - the 'ultimate aim' of German policy - was forced emigration, to be encouraged 'by all possible means'. Heydrich was empowered to establish a Central Office for Jewish Emigration, similar to the one in Vienna, and to run it to ensure that, within a decade, Germany would be free of Jews. While some 150,000 Jews had left Germany between March 1933 and November 1938, government efforts to 'encourage' emigration had been implemented only half-heartedly. Now, emigration was to be handled in a rigorous and centralised fashion.

Heydrich, however, faced several problems. Given that many Jews had already left, those who remained were generally the elderly and the unskilled, for whom there was no great demand abroad. Some countries, not wanting to have thousands of Jews dumped on them, had tightened their rules of admission. Britain, faced with heightened hostility between Jews and Arabs, was determined to limit Jewish immigration to Palestine.

Despite the obstacles, the Central Office, applying the techniques used by Eichmann in Austria, was generally successful. Some 150,000

Jews left Germany in the twelve months after November 1938. Most went to European countries (including Britain); others went to North, South and Central America, Australia, and Palestine. The increase in emigration was partly the result of SS policy, partly the result of countries like Britain and France showing sympathy to the German Jews' plight, and partly the result of an understandably greater willingness to emigrate on the part of Jews themselves. In early 1939, high-level German civil servants had talks with British and American officials in an effort to ensure that there were countries willing to take Jewish emigrants. Hitler's hopes that Britain might agree to some remote African territory becoming a Jewish colony never materialised. Meanwhile Heydrich and the SS supported emigration to Palestine.

9 Conclusion

Functionalist historians (like Mommsen) see Nazi anti-Jewish policy between 1933 and 1939 as erratic and improvised. They believe that Hitler had no very clear idea of what should be done with Jews, apart from turning them into pariahs and think he was perfectly prepared to fall in with whatever 'solution' to the Jewish problem was currently in vogue. But other historians (like Saul Friedländer) believe - more persuasively - that Nazi goals had been systematically pursued and rapidly achieved. (For example, by September 1939 some 70 per cent of Germany's Jews had been driven to emigrate.) Moreover, most Holocaust historians think that Hitler was the principal - if not always the sole - driving force of anti-Semitism in the Nazi movement. In Marrus's opinion: 'Hitler alone defined the Jewish menace with the authority, consistency and ruthlessness needed to fix its place for the Party and later the Reich.'[11] Party activists, who urged him to take even more radical action against the Jews, urged him in a direction he wanted to go. Their influence should not be exaggerated: they never compelled Hitler to take major steps he did not want to take.

In Hitler's view, just as it was impossible for a leopard to change its spots, so it was impossible for there ever to be such a thing as a good Jew. The logical conclusion of such thinking was the 'elimination' of Jews from Germany. For much of the period 1933-9 Hitler had shown that he was prepared to be pragmatic, taking into account internal and external pressures, in pursuing his ends. However, belief in certain principles and skill at tactical manoeuvring are by no means mutually exclusive. By 1938 Hitler's domestic and international position was much stronger. The marked increase in anti-Semitic activity after 1937 may well have reflected Germany's growing power, Hitler's growing contempt for international opinion, and the fact that the conservative old guard within Germany had gone. Precisely where Hitler's anti-Jewish policy was leading by 1939 is thus a subject of much debate. Hitler's speech to the Reichstag in January 1939 was certainly threatening.

I In the course of my life I have often been a prophet, and have usually been ridiculed for it. During the time of my struggle for power it was in the first instance only the Jewish race that received my prophecies with laughter when I said that I would one day take over the leadership of
5 the State ... and that I would then among other things settle the Jewish problem. Their laughter was uproarious, but I think that for some time now they have been laughing on the other side of their face. Today I will once more be a prophet: if the international Jewish financiers in and outside Europe should succeed in plunging the nations once more into
10 a world war, then the result will not be the Bolshevizing of the earth, and thus the victory of Jewry, but the annihilation of the Jewish race in Europe.[12]

The fact that Hitler expressed such violent intentions cannot be taken as proof that he was already set on genocide. Indeed, given that Germany's 'ultimate aim' in 1939 was forced emigration, it seems unlikely that he was contemplating mass murder. Yet, the radical nature of Nazi anti-Semitism was such that completion of one stage often entailed the start of another - more militant - stage. And, as Hitler made clear in the Reichstag speech, the outbreak of another war was likely to put the Jews in great danger. Nevertheless, while the possibility of genocide may have been in Hitler's mind, it is impossible to prove that his set objective in 1939 (or before) was to exterminate all Germany's - never mind all Europe's - Jews.

References

1 J. Noakes and G. Pridham (eds), *Nazism 1919-1945: 2: State, Economy and Society 1933-1939* (University of Exeter, 1984), p. 523.
2 Hermann Graml, *Anti-Semitism in the Third Reich* (Blackwell, 1992), p. 91.
3 Ibid, p. 92.
4 Saul Friedländer, *Nazi Germany and the Jews: The Years of Persecution 1933-39* (Weidenfeld and Nicolson, 1997), p.12.
5 Philippe Burrin, *Hitler and the Jews: The Genesis of the Holocaust* (Edward Arnold, 1989), p. 51.
6 Noakes and Pridham (eds), *Nazism 1919-1945*, 2, p. 550.
7 Ibid, p. 555-6
8 Hermann Graml, *Anti-Semitism in the Third Reich*, p. 28.
9 Ibid, p.28.
10 Noakes and Pridham (eds), *Nazism 1919-1945*, 2, p. 558.
11 Michael R. Marrus, *The Holocaust in History* (Penguin, 1987), p. 17.
12 J. Noakes and G. Pridham (eds), *Nazism 1919-1945: 3: Foreign Policy, War and Racial Extermination* (University of Exeter, 1988), p. 1049.

Answering essay questions on 'Anti-Semitism in Action: 1933-39'

Consider the following question:

'To what extent did Adolf Hitler control Nazi anti-Semitic policy in the period 1933-9 and to what extent was that policy erratic and improvised?'

Perhaps the most important - and difficult - part of any essay is the introduction. It is your first opportunity to impress (or depress) the marker and is usually the key to a successful essay. While there is no perfect way of writing an introductory paragraph, there are certain things you ought to be trying to do:

a) You should be explaining the meaning of the set question. This involves defining the most important terms in the title and also identifying the periods of time which are relevant. These are vital issues. If you understand the question you are well on the way to answering it. You will thus avoid the worst trap of all - answering a different question from the one set!

b) You should be identifying the key areas within the question that will be addressed in more detail later in the essay.

c) You should already be formulating your argument. Remember that you should answer a question right from the start of an essay. It is a waste of time and space simply to say that you are going to answer the question. Of course that is what you are going to do - so get on and do it!

d) Avoid spending too long setting the scene in a general way, by giving too much background information. This can easily lead into narrative. Narrative answers rarely get to grips with the analytical questions normally set in exams or for coursework.

e) Remember that a good first paragraph leads in to the rest of the essay. It is, in many ways, an essay in miniature. It should outline the main issues which will then form paragraph points for the rest of the essay.

Try and write a first paragraph for the essay question above. Can you think of a good opening sentence? Make sure you clarify the relevant issues. What overall argument will you put forward? It is likely that your answer will be a qualified yes or no. Yes ... in this way Hitler was weak/Nazi policy was improvised. No ... in this way Hitler was in control/Nazi policy was not erratic. Try and reach a conclusion to your essay before you start writing the introduction!

Summary Diagram
Anti-Semitism in Action: 1933-9

VIOLENCE		LEGAL MEASURES
	1933	
		Boycott of Jewish goods (April)
Revolution from below (March)		Law for Restoration of Professional Civil Service (April)
	1934	
CALM		CALM
	1935	
		Nuremberg Laws (September)
Attacks on synagogues and Jewish shops (spring and summer)		First Supplementary Decree to Reich Citizenship Law (November)
	1936	
CALM		CALM
O L Y M P I C		G A M E S
	1937	
CALM		CALM
	1938	Aryanisation
Violence in Austria (March)		Decree for Registration of Jewish Properties (April)
Kristallnacht (November)		Compulsory Aryanisation of
Hitler's Reichstag threat (January)	1939	Jewish businesses (January)

1. Hitler's views: 1937 and 1939
Read the extracts from Hitler's speeches on page 43 and page 50. Answer the following questions:
- **a)** What action does Hitler suggest he may take against the Jews i) in 1937 ii) in 1939? (4 marks)
- **b)** What may have been Hitler's purpose for speaking as he did i) in 1937 ii) in 1939? (6 marks)
- **c)** Do these speeches prove that Hitler was set upon exterminating German Jews? (5 marks)

2. Anti-Semitic Activity in 1933 and 1938
Read the extracts from the American consul on page 35 and pages 46-7 . Answer the following questions:
- **a)** According to the two sources, what seem to have been i) the main differences and ii) the main similarities between the anti-Semitic action in 1933 and that in 1938? (5 marks)
- **b)** What evidence does the American consul cite to suggest that the events of Kristallnacht were not 'spontaneous'? (4 marks)
- **c)** Would you consider the American consul to be a reliable source? Explain your answer. (6 marks)

4 The Effect of War: 1939-41

1 Introduction

On 1 September 1939 Hitler invaded Poland and two days later found himself at war with France and Britain and in alliance with the USSR - a position that was the opposite of what he wished. The subsequent three-week annihilation of Poland freed him from immediate danger on his eastern flank and allowed him to concentrate his forces in the west. In 1940 German forces overran Denmark, Norway, Holland, Belgium and France. So assured did Germany's final victory seem that Italy now joined the war on Germany's side. By July 1940, therefore, Hitler was the master of Europe. Only Britain still held out against him and it seemed only a matter of time before it made peace or was conquered.

The outbreak of war in September 1939 represented a watershed in Nazi policies towards the Jews. Hitler believed that Jews had been responsible for Germany's defeat in the First World War. 'A November 1918 will never again be repeated in the history of Germany', Hitler proclaimed in his first wartime speech. The lives of German soldiers were far more valuable than the lives of 'traitors to the fatherland'. The fact that Hitler held such views was obviously a huge threat to Germany's Jewish population. The Jewish threat to Germany, by contrast, was insignificant. By 1939 there were fewer than 200,000 Jews still in Germany. However, Germany's success in 1939-40 resulted in a dramatic increase in the number of Jews under Nazi control. In the German-controlled areas of Poland alone, there were some two million Jews. The 'Jewish problem' thus assumed a new dimension.

Nazi Jewish policy from September 1939 to early 1941 seems to have been largely improvised. Little had been planned before 1939; given the constantly changing conditions thereafter, nothing was inevitable. Until June 1941 Germany was not at war with either the USSR or the USA. Hitler, in consequence, could not ignore 'world' opinion. The evidence suggests that until 1941 he did not envisage - let alone order - a full-scale extermination programme. Nevertheless, there is no doubt that the outbreak of war created a new and brutalised context for dealing with the 'Jewish problem'. Moreover, the introduction (in 1939) of a euthanasia programme for Germany's severely handicapped did not bode well for the fate of European Jews.

2 German and West European Jews

The outbreak of war resulted in more discriminatory measures against Jews. German Jews had driving licences, radios and telephones confiscated and were subject to curfew orders. They were not issued with clothing coupons and their food ration cards were stamped with a large J. Goebbels continued to press for harsher anti-Semitic measures and wanted all Jews to wear the Star of David so they could be clearly identified. Hitler opposed this - for now. But all violations by Jews of the discriminatory regulations resulted in draconian punishment.

The outbreak of war, and the fact that most sea lanes were now closed to German vessels, complicated the problem of Jewish emigration, which still remained the priority of the Nazi regime. However, by 1940 the establishment of Jewish reservations in Poland (see page 59) or France seemed possible. From July 1940, over 20,000 Jews were deported from Alsace and Lorraine (annexed by Germany from France) and other parts of western Germany to camps in southern France. The deportees were forced to leave behind most of their belongings. Conditions in the French camps were poor and many Jews died from disease. However, protests from the French Vichy government, which did not wish to see France used as a dumping ground for German Jews, brought an end to the 'French solution'.

Hitler seems to have had no clear idea of what to do with the Jews in the occupied countries of western Europe. In many places the Germans imposed discriminatory ordinances or leaned on 'friendly' governments, like those in Slovakia and Hungary, to do so. But there were no massacres. Nor were Jews forced into ghettos. Several German agencies were responsible for Jewish policy in western Europe. These included the Foreign Ministry, military and civilian occupation authorities and various branches of the SS, not least the Reich Security Central Office (or RSHA), established in September 1939 and combining the *Gestapo* and the SD. While the SS claimed pre-eminence in Jewish policy, the other branches of the Nazi government opposed giving Himmler a totally free hand - with some success. Given that racial policy was not a central concern of many of these agencies, anti-Jewish policies in western Europe tended towards caution.

3 The Madagascar Plan

In the summer of 1940 Heydrich, anxious to find a 'territorial final solution', asked the German Foreign Ministry to find a suitable dumping place for Jews. By July 1940 the Foreign Ministry had begun to promote the notion of sending Jews to the French colony of Madagascar, an island 250 miles off the south-east coast of Africa. The idea of using Madagascar as a Jewish reservation had been considered by anti-Semites across Europe for many years. The defeat of France and the likely surrender of Britain in 1940 suddenly made the Madagascar plan feasible and there was apparent enthusiasm for the project at every level, from Hitler downwards. According to the Foreign Ministry plan, the island would be largely administered by

Jews, but under the overall jurisdiction of Himmler.

The Madagascar plan was far from humane. The Nazis anticipated that many Jews would die on the journey or as a result of the inhospitable climate when they arrived. The notion that the Jews should be left to rot in Madagascar was not far from the surface. In the event, however, the continuation of the war with Britain and British control of the sea, ensured that the plan was never realised. Nevertheless, it remained the 'final solution' well into 1941.

4 The Situation in Poland

a) German Rule

The German conquest of Poland was to have dire consequences for Poles in general and for Polish Jews in particular. Hitler made his brutal intentions abundantly clear from the start. In August 1939 a special 2,700-strong task force - or *Einsatzgruppen* - was set up, composed of men from various police and SS units. The *Einsatzgruppen*'s role was to combat 'all anti-German elements in enemy territory' and to 'render harmless' the leadership class in Poland. Following closely behind the advancing German army, *Einsatzgruppen* forces executed thousands of Polish doctors, teachers, lawyers and landowners.

By the end of September 1939 Poland was defeated. By the terms of the Nazi-Soviet Pact of August 1939 (which was revised in late September), Germany acquired 188,000 sq. kms of Polish territory, containing a population comprising over 17 million Poles, 2 million Jews and 675,000 Germans. At first military authorities ruled this newly conquered area. But in early October 1939 Himmler was appointed 'Reich Commissar for the Consolidation of German Nationhood' (RFKD), responsible for settling Germans in the conquered territories and also for 'excluding the damaging influence of those foreign sections of the population which pose a danger to the Reich and the German national community'.[1] Even after Poland's surrender, Himmler let the *Einsatzgruppen* massacre large numbers of Poles. Many army leaders disliked the killings and were anxious to escape responsibility for them. General Blaskowitz, the supreme commander in the east, was prompted to write to Hitler in November 1939:

1 The attitude of the troops towards the SS and the police fluctuates between revulsion and hatred. Every soldier feels sickened and repelled by the crimes being perpetrated in Poland by men from the Reich representing the state authorities. The men fail to understand how such
5 things - which happen, so to speak, under their aegis - can go unpunished.[2]

But Hitler's sympathies were with the SS and police. War, he said, could not be waged by 'Salvation Army methods', and proceeded to grant an amnesty to the killers. So clear was Hitler's position that army officers quickly put aside any qualms of a professional or moral nature, and criticisms of the atrocities came to an end. In November 1939 Hitler freed the army from virtually any role in the administration of Poland. The army leadership washed its hands of the matter and turned with relief to preparing the operations in the west.

Meanwhile Germany incorporated directly into the Reich about half of the conquered Polish territory. The annexed area (the so-called 'incorporated territories') was inhabited by some 10 million people, 80 per cent of whom were Poles. Under the new arrangement the German provinces of East Prussia and Silesia were extended and two new *Reichsgau* - Danzig-West Prussia and Posen (renamed Warthegau in 1940) - were set up. The remaining German-occupied Polish territory was not incorporated into the Reich. Hitler envisaged that this area - soon known as the 'General Government' - would become a dumping ground for Poles, Jews and Gypsies, under German control and serving German needs.

Himmler had a clear view of what his task was: 'Our duty in the East is not Germanisation in the former sense of the term, that is, imposing German language and laws upon the population, but to ensure that only people of pure German blood inhabit the East.' His first priority was settling some 200,000 ethnic Germans from the USSR, Estonia and Latvia in the incorporated territories. He faced even more pressure in 1940 when the German government agreed to repatriate large numbers of ethnic Germans from the General Government, Lithuania, Bessarabia and Romania. SS racial experts carefully scrutinised potential settlers with regard to their Nordic blood and would-be immigrants were also medically examined to check for signs of hereditary illness or deformity.

To make room for the ethnic Germans, Himmler set about deporting Poles and Jews from the incorporated territories to the General Government. Families were given only a few minutes to move out and had to leave most of their belongings for the incoming German settlers. Those who objected were liable to be summarily executed. Those Poles who were young and fit might find themselves sent to Germany to work as slave labourers, but most were forced onto trains and dumped in the General Government. In a May 1940 memorandum Himmler accepted that deportation could be 'cruel and tragic'. But he went on to write that 'the method [deportation] is still the mildest and best, if one rejects the Bolshevik method of physical extermination of a people ... as un-German and impossible'.[3] By the end of 1940, some 300,000 Poles and Jews had been deported from the incorporated territories. The Poles and Jews who remained were subject to massive discrimination and oppression. At any time they could be driven from their homes and farms to make way for ethnic Germans. All Polish secondary schools and most primary schools were closed. So were most Polish churches. Poles were denied the right to enter any profession.

b) The General Government

In October 1939 Hans Frank became governor of the General Government. On paper, Frank seemed to have absolute power. But the reality was different. One limitation was the shortage of German officials. Another was the fact that within the General Government, the SS, operating largely independently of Frank, succeeded in estab-lishing a virtual state within a state to a greater extent than anywhere else in German-occupied Europe. This came about for two reasons. Firstly, the SS had major police powers: SS-police could consign people to concentration camps without trial and shoot anyone committing a violent act against the Reich. Secondly, the SS had a vital role in Nazi re-settlement plans.

German policy in the General Government varied from exploita-tion and discrimination to some aspects of rebuilding, and even accommodation with Poles. But terror was the usual order of the day. In May 1940 the German authorities began a new 'pacification' policy to wipe out potentially rebellious elements. Teachers, clergy, doctors, businessmen, landowners and academics who had survived the 1939 killings were either shot or sent to labour camps which sprang up all over the General Government. From October 1939 all Poles aged between 18 and 60 within the General Government were subject to compulsory public labour. At this stage, it was assumed that most Poles would work in the General Government itself. But by January 1940 Germany was desperately short of workers. Having failed to recruit enough Polish volunteers, the Germans resorted to force. Cinemas, churches and sometimes whole districts were suddenly surrounded by the police and suitable people rounded up and sent to Germany. By the summer of 1941, there were about three million foreign workers in Germany, the majority of whom were Poles.

5 Polish Jews

In Hitler's view both Poles and Jews counted as vermin which had to be cleared from prospective German living space. But Hitler saw a critical distinction between the two groups. While Poles were low on the evolu-tionary ladder, Jews posed a deadly danger to Germany and to mankind. In 1939 Jews comprised some 10 per cent of the Polish population. Some 1,270,000 lived in the General Government, while 630,000 lived in the incorporated territories. The Polish Jews possessed a strong religious and ethnic consciousness. They were clearly different from Poles. Indeed most Poles were strongly anti-Semitic.

Control of so many Jews meant that the Nazis now had the real prospect of ridding Europe of a major element of the 'Jewish menace'. However, there is no hard evidence that Hitler contemplated genocide pre-1941. Hitler still had to consider the views of the USA and USSR. Given Hitler's (mistaken) belief that Jews were all-powerful in the USSR, a genocidal onslaught against the Polish Jews might well have sparked a war with the USSR before Germany was ready. Mass Jewish slaughter might also have driven the USA into the British camp.

However, if Hitler was not yet ready to approve genocidal policies, Polish Jews still suffered terrible discrimination and persecution. Synagogues were burned and there was large-scale, if unsystematic, expropriation of Jewish property. Although the *Einsatzgruppen* had no specific orders to execute Jews, they took it upon themselves to shoot large numbers as they set about wiping out the Polish intelligentsia. In mid-September a special SS task force carried out mass shootings of Jews in Upper Silesia with the aim of driving them into the neighbouring Russian-occupied area.

While the conquest of Poland meant that Germany had a far greater Jewish problem, the conquest also offered a solution. Leading Nazis quickly realised that there was a possibility of creating a vast reservation for all European Jews in the General Government. The following are from the minutes of a meeting of Heydrich and his RSHA department heads on 27 September 1939:

1   The deportation of the Jews to the [General Government] ... has been approved by the Führer. However, the whole process is to take place over a period of one year. ...
     The Jews are to be brought together in ghettos in the cities in order
5   to ensure a better chance of controlling them and later of removing them.[4]

By the end of September 1939 it was provisionally decided that Jews and other undesirables should be sent to the Lublin district - the furthest corner of the German empire. Deportations of Jews from the incorporated territories were to have priority and to be completed by February 1940. Implementation of the plan was delayed for a time, partly to await Britain and France's response to Hitler's peace offer made in October 1939. That same month, however, Adolf Eichmann jumped the gun and, without proper authorisation, set about transporting Jews from Vienna, Upper Silesia and Bohemia and Moravia to a rural area near Nisko, part of the district of Lublin. Some of the first arrivals constructed a makeshift camp but the majority of those transported were simply driven into the countryside and literally ordered to get lost. Complaints from the army about the resultant chaos prompted the RSHA to call a halt to the Nisko transports on 26 October 1939.

Official mass Jewish deportation from the incorporated territories did not get under way until December 1939. Thousands of Jews, stripped of everything they possessed, were crammed into freight cars and deposited in the Lublin area. However, Himmler's drive to move all the Jews from the incorporated territories was nowhere near completion by February 1940. By then, his deportation operation had run up against the objections of Frank and Goering.

Throughout 1939 Frank had issued a series of draconian measures against Jews in the General Government. In November they were forced to wear (on pain of death) a white armband bearing the star of David. Jews had to salute all Nazi personnel. In December they were prevented from changing their abode without permission. Two years' forced labour was made compulsory for all Jewish males. However, Frank had no wish for the General Government to be the depository for everyone else's Jews. In February 1940 he complained to Goering (who still had overall responsibility for the Jewish question) about the problems caused by having to absorb thousands of Jewish refugees and asked him to halt the deportations. Goering, concerned at the economic disruption the deportations were causing, was receptive to Frank's argument. Accordingly, in March 1940, he ordered an end to all evacuations, except those approved by Frank. Himmler reluctantly agreed to suspend all further deportations until August. For the time being, at least, his grandiose demographic ambitions had failed. The speed with which Nazi leaders seized upon the Madagascar plan is perhaps a measure of the frustration that had built up over the problem of demographic engineering in Poland. While Frank escaped an immediate deluge of Jews, small-scale deportations of Jews and Gypsies to the Lublin area continued. By March 1941, however, transportation problems (arising from the German build-up for the attack on Russia) resulted in all re-settlement plans being postponed.

6 The Polish Ghettos

The concentration and isolation of Jews in Polish cities as a prepara-tory move to their eventual expulsion further east became part of Nazi policy in September 1939. However, the exact nature of the 'ghettoisation' policy from 1939 to 1941, like so many other aspects of Nazi anti-Jewish policy, has been the subject of conflicting interpreta-tions. Intentionalists think the policy was a conscious preliminary step for total annihilation. Functionalists, while accepting that ghettoisa-tion eventually did facilitate the implementation of the Holocaust, believe that the Nazi leadership had not really thought through its policies. American historian Christopher Browning, while not regarding himself as a functionalist, is certain that there was no master ghettoisation plan in September 1939, or for many months thereafter. Nor is he convinced that ghettoisation was ever designed to decimate the Jews. He has shown that ghettoisation was carried out at different times in different ways for different reasons on the initia-tive of different local authorities.

In 1939 most Polish cities already had large Jewish populations. Although there had been no deliberate ghettoisation policy for decades, most cities had Jewish areas. The German process of forced ghettoisation only began to be implemented during 1940. One major reason for establishing the ghettos was to prevent the spread of disease. Some German doctors and health officials believed that Jews, as a result of their culture and nature, were carriers of various diseases (especially spotted fever). While not the only people advocating ghettoisation, doctors may have played a decisive role in some towns in bringing it about.

The first Jewish 'sealed' ghetto was established in Lodz, once the second largest city in Poland but now in the Warthegau, in April 1940. The chief German administrator of the Lodz district was Friedrich Ubelhor. In December 1939 he expressed his general understanding of the situation: 'The creation of the ghetto is, of course, only a provisional measure. I reserve for myself the decision as to the point in time and the means by which the ghetto ... will be cleared of Jews. The final goal, at any rate, must be to lance this festering boil.'[5] Most German administrators in the east probably thought similarly. However, as a result of the failure of the Lublin deportation plan, the ghettos lasted much longer than was initially anticipated.

On Heydrich's orders, Jews had to establish their own councils (or *Judenrat*) in the ghettos. These councils, predominantly composed of middle-class and professional Jews, had some local power and were supposed to maintain 'an orderly community life'. But essentially their function was to carry out the orders of the German authorities. One important task was compiling lists of the number of people in the ghettos. Another was to recruit workers for forced labour battalions, which operated both within the ghettos and in labour camps outside. At first the ghettos gave a false sense of security. Given that there was virtually no contact between Jews and gentiles, there was less intimidation. In Lodz, the chairman of the Jewish council, Chaim Rumkovski, established himself as effective dictator of the 150,000-strong Jewish community. Currency was issued with his signature and stamps printed bearing his likeness.

Warsaw experienced ghettoisation in fits and starts. Not until March 1940 was the Jewish council told to begin construction - at its own expense - of a 2.2 metre-high wall around the Jewish quarter. The ghetto (not finally sealed until November 1940) soon housed about 500,000 Jews - over 100,000 people per sq. km. This resulted in 15 people sharing an average apartment and six people sharing an average room. Only one per cent of Warsaw apartments had running water. Once economic ties with the outside world were broken, supplies were quickly exhausted. In Warsaw, the meagre food rations for Jews eventually fell below an average of 300 calories a day (compared with 634 calories for Poles and 2,310 for Germans). Heating materials were also in very short supply. In consequence, the health of the vast majority steadily deteriorated. Ironically (and accidentally: it was not the result of a diabolical Nazi plan) ghettoisation

The photographs on this page and on page 63 were taken by Heinrich Jost, a German army sergeant whose unit was billeted near Warsaw. He visited the ghetto on 19 September 1941. His entry was strictly against regulations, as was his use of a camera. But he was wearing his Wehrmacht *uniform and no one challenged him. He wandered through the ghetto streets, taking pictures as he went. The photographs were not shown to anyone until the 1980s*

in Warsaw resulted in the spotted fever epidemic that German doctors had feared. Typhus and TB also flourished.

The following description of life in the Warsaw ghetto is taken from the diary of a visitor, Stanislav Rozycki:

1   On the streets children are crying in vain, children who are dying of hunger. They howl, beg, sing, moan, shiver with cold, without underwear, without clothing, without shoes, in rags, sacks, flannel which are bound in strips round the emaciated skeletons, children swollen with hunger,
5   disfigured, half conscious, already completely grown-up at the age of five, gloomy and weary of life. ... Ten per cent of the new generation have already perished ...

     There are not only children. Young and old people, men and women, bourgeois and proletarians, intelligentsia and business people are being
10 declassed and degraded. ... They are being gobbled up by the streets on which they are brutally and ruthlessly thrown. They beg for one month, for two months, for three months - but they all go down-hill and die on the streets or in hospitals from cold, or hunger, or sickness, or depression ...

15   For various reasons standards of hygiene are terribly poor. Above all, the fearful population density in the streets with which nowhere in Europe can be remotely compared. ... And then the lack of light, gas and heating materials. Water consumption is also much reduced: people wash themselves much less and do not have baths or hot water. There
20 are no green spaces, gardens, parks: no clumps of trees and no lawns to be seen ...

     People eat what is available, however much is available and when it is available. Other principles of nutrition are unknown here. Having said all this, one can easily draw one's own conclusions as to the consequences:
25 stomach typhus and typhus, dysentery, tuberculosis, pneumonia, influenza, metabolic disturbances, the most common digestive illnesses, lack of vitamins and all other illnesses associated with the lack of bread, fresh air, clothing and heating materials. ...

     The hospitals are so terribly over-crowded that there are 2-3
30 patients lying in every bed. Those who do not find a place in a bed lie on the floor in rooms and corridors. The shortage of the necessary medicines ... makes it impossible to treat the sick.[6]

The following are the monthly death figures for the Jewish ghetto in Warsaw in 1941:[7]

January	898
February	1,023
March	1,608
April	2,061
May	3,821
June	4,290
July	5,550

August	5,560
September	4,545
October	4,716
November	4,801
December	4,239

Hitler's government, refusing to acknowledge that the Lublin resettlement plan had collapsed, issued few directives. Thus, German authorities in Warsaw, Lodz and other cities were left to cope as best they could until Berlin decided what to do. (Sealed ghettos in Cracow and Lublin were not established until 1941.) The German managers, while not necessarily fanatical anti-Semites, were loyal Nazis, committed to their careers and to doing their duty. Some managers thought that the Jews should be simply left to die. (Browning calls these 'attritionists'.) But others advocated creating a viable ghetto economy, which would allow the Jews to maintain themselves for an indefinite period. (Browning calls these 'productionists'.[8]) This necessitated giving the Jewish communities subsidies to enable them to start work. The 'productionists' claimed that it would be in Germany's best interests if the Jews became self-sufficient and helped the German war economy.

In most Polish cities, including Warsaw and Lodz, the 'productionists' prevailed over the 'attritionists'. They were assisted by Jewish leaders who hoped that hard-working, productive Jewish communities might make themselves so indispensable to the Nazi war effort that they might be spared further torment. (Some spoke of 'salvation through work'.) Nevertheless, immense problems still stood in the way of turning the ghettos into productive entities. Even the most enthusiastic 'productionists' accepted that the ghettos were destined for liquidation at some time in the future. Thus no great priority was given to them and food and fuel shortages continued. But in Lodz and Warsaw ghetto conditions did begin to improve and the death rate fell. Interestingly, the German managers in Lodz and Warsaw acted along different lines. Those in Lodz tried to control the economy - with some success. By the summer of 1941, around 40,000 Jews were producing goods like furniture and shoes. In Warsaw, on the other hand, the German authorities tended to leave matters to the Jews themselves - similarly successfully. Production of a wide variety of goods rose sharply. Frustrated ghetto managers, therefore, did not turn to mass murder in 1941-2 as a way to resolve their economic and social difficulties. The Holocaust actually destroyed economic experiments that were just beginning to bear fruit. It was renewed intervention from Berlin that brought about an abrupt change of policy, not local improvisation. Browning is convinced that the German managers' behaviour does not indicate the existence of any premeditated plan for mass murder.

Not all Polish Jews were confined to ghettos. Many were sent to work in labour camps away from their families. Without adequate tools, food, clothing and medical provision, workers were forced to do hard physical labour such as building railways, draining marshes and building fortifications. Historians estimate that some 500-600,000 Polish Jews died in the ghettos and labour camps in 1939-41.

Nazi propaganda images of Polish Jews helped reinforce the notion among Germans that Jews were profoundly alien. In Poland Jews had not been assimilated into Polish life: many could not speak Polish. Living more or less apart and following strict orthodox rules in matters of dress and custom, they seemed to conform to the stereotype of the 'eternal Jew'. When this alien quality was combined with the deterioration of the Jewish community, as a result of Nazi policies, Jews increasingly approximated to the Nazi images of them as sub-humans and 'carriers of disease and corruption'.

7 Euthanasia

Meanwhile Hitler had embarked on another policy which was to have major repercussions for Jews - euthanasia. The euthanasia programme was a euphemism to camouflage the killing of mentally and physically handicapped people deemed to be 'unworthy of life'. The aim was partly financial: euthanasia would help conserve resources, making more doctors and hospital beds available for wounded soldiers. But Hitler's determination to create a pure and healthy race was probably more important than economic considerations. Many Germans shared Hitler's ideological convictions. Well before 1939, many institutions had already cut the costs of caring for their mental patients and there was also a marked decline in sense of duty among the medical staff. Indeed there is some evidence that a number of psychiatric patients were effectively murdered in hospitals from as early as 1933. From 1939 Hitler felt secure enough to kill on a much greater and more systematic scale.

Hitler and his subordinates did not slither accidentally into the euthanasia programme. Nor did bureaucratic mechanisms assume a life of their own in a way that some historians imagine was the case with the Holocaust. The euthanasia programme was a carefully planned operation with clear objectives.

a) Children's Euthanasia

In 1938 the Knauer family petitioned Hitler for permission to have their terribly deformed child 'put to sleep'. This petition reached Hitler through his private Chancellery, headed by Philipp Bouhler, where similar appeals had already been collected. Hitler decided to act. Instructing his personal doctor Karl Brandt to visit the Knauer infant, Hitler told him to kill the child if his diagnosis agreed with the conditions outlined in the petition. Brandt duly confirmed the diagnosis and the child was secretly killed. According to Hans Hefelmann, giving evidence in a post-war trial:

> The Knauer case prompted Hitler to authorise Brandt and Bouhler to deal with similar cases in the same way as with the Knauer child. I cannot say whether or not this authorisation was given orally or in writing. In any event, Brandt did not show us a written authorisation.[9]

Suspecting that children's euthanasia might be unpopular, Hitler insisted that it be treated as top secret. Between February and May 1939 Bouhler, Viktor Brack (the day-to-day manager of the programme) and a small team of doctors and bureaucrats (including Hefelmann) worked out the methods of implementation. The planners fabricated a fictitious organisation to camouflage their activities - the 'Reich Committee for the Scientific Registration of Serious Hereditary and Congenitally-based Ailments' - shortened to 'Reich Committee'. In August 1939 a decree ordered midwives and doctors to report all infants born with severe medical conditions. Doctors were also to report all children below the age of three with serious conditions. Forms were to be returned to the Reich Committee. The impression was given that this information would be used for medical research. The decree did not reveal the actual reasons for the requirement to report handicapped children.

The medical experts on the Reich Committee based their decisions to kill or not to kill solely on the reporting forms. They never saw children in the flesh. Those children selected to die were transferred, supposedly for expert care, to special paediatric clinics. The first was at Brandenburg-Gorden, a large hospital near Berlin. Killings began here in the early autumn of 1939. Eventually over 20 killing wards were established by the Reich Committee. The euthanasia programme depended not only on the co-operation of bureaucrats and doctors, but also on parents who had to agree to surrender their children to the special wards. This usually posed no problem. Some parents genuinely believed that their children would receive the best treatment possible. Others were more suspicious. But there was little that they could - or in many cases wanted to - do. Many parents were delighted that the authorities had freed them from the burden of raising a disabled child.

While actually ordering the killing, the Reich Committee did not care how the children died. Doctors were left to find the best method. Some simply let the children starve to death. But most preferred to give drug overdoses, sometimes in tablet form, sometimes by injection. Altogether, some 5,000 severely handicapped children were probably killed in Germany during the Second World War.

b) Adult Euthanasia

Probably the first killings of adult psychiatric patients began in

September 1939 in occupied Poland. Polish inmates of mental asylums were simply shot by SS execution squads. By November 1939 over 4,000 people had been killed and a special SS unit continued the killing over the winter of 1939-40. Some Polish mental patients were locked in a large van into which carbon monoxide gas was then pumped. Fifty people at a time could be killed in this way. These actions, however, were distinct from the official euthanasia killings.

At some time in the early autumn of 1939 (there is conflicting evidence about the exact date) Hitler initiated the policy of killing German handicapped adults. Bouhler and Brandt quickly convinced Hitler that their organisation, which was already planning children's euthanasia, should also undertake the adult version. Given that the killing would be on a much greater scale than the operation against children, maintaining secrecy (a major concern) would not be easy. Another problem facing the euthanasia team was how to convince co-operating professionals, especially doctors, that they would not be prosecuted for killing patients. Hitler, concerned about negative world and German opinion, resisted all attempts to introduce a euthanasia law. However, he did sign a document (in October 1939), written on his personal notepaper and dated 1 September, empowering 'specific doctors' to grant 'a mercy death' to those suffering from illnesses deemed to be 'incurable'. Copies of Hitler's authorisation were shown to prospective collaborators.

Those involved in planning adult euthanasia realised the need to create an organisation that could, like the Reich Committee, serve as a front to hide the fact of the killings. A central office was eventually established in Berlin at Tiergarten Strasse No. 4. Soon the adult euthanasia programme was known as Operation T-4 or simply as T-4. The daily management of the programme was left to Brack, who zealously executed his new duties.

The T-4 programme soon had several offices. The medical office supervised the collection of data on patients, and appointed and instructed doctors and nurses assigned to the killing centres. An administrative office co-ordinated the efforts to hide the killings. This involved misleading both the relatives of the victims and the various agencies involved in treating handicapped patients. The transport office arranged for the transfer of patients to the killing centres.

In September 1939 a decree bound all public, religious and private institutions holding mental patients to provide specific information as follows:

1   All patients must be reported who
   i)   Suffer from the following illnesses and cannot be employed in the asylum except in mechanical tasks (e.g. plucking etc):
        Schizophrenia, epilepsy ... senile illnesses, paralysis not responsive
5   to therapy ... feeble-mindedness of all kinds. ...
   ii)   have been in asylums continuously for at least five years or

iii)   are confined as criminal lunatics or
iv)   do not possess German nationality - or are not of German or
      related blood.[10]

Little space was provided on the forms for details about the individuals' condition. Nevertheless, the forms were collated at the T-4
offices in Berlin where a panel of three 'experts' decided - on the
basis of scant information - who should live and who should die.
Scores of decisions were made daily and the assessors were paid
according to the number of forms they processed. One doctor
decided on the life and death of 15,000 patients in a nine-month
period during which he was also working full-time in a psychiatric
clinic. Once patients were selected for death, they were transferred to
the killing wards. The transfers were disguised as relocations due to
war emergency. Even the surrendering institutions did not at first
know the purpose of the transfers. Relatives were informed only after
the victims had been 'transferred'.

Killings got under way in the autumn of 1939 at Grafeneck, near
Stuttgart. At first most patients were murdered either by a drug over-
dose or by gradual starvation. But T-4 doctors soon decided that
carbon monoxide gassing was a more efficient killing method. The
first demonstration of gassing took place at the Brandenburg asylum
in January 1940. Dr August Becker, a chemist, reported after the war
as follows:

1   I was ordered by Brack to attend the first euthanasia experiment in the
    Brandenburg asylum near Berlin. ... There was a room similar to a
    shower room which was approximately 3 metres by 5 metres and 3
    metres high and tiled. There were benches round the room and a water
5   pipe about one inch in diameter ran along the wall about 10 cm off the
    floor. There were small holes in this pipe from which the carbon
    monoxide gas poured out. ... There was a rectangular peephole in the
    entrance door ... through which the delinquents could be observed. ...
    For this first gassing about 18-20 people were led into this 'shower
10 room' by the nursing staff. These men had to undress in an anteroom
    until they were completely naked. The doors were shut behind them.
    They went quietly into the room and showed no signs of being upset.
    Dr Widmann operated the gas. I could see through the peephole that
    after about a minute the people had collapsed or lay on the benches.
15 There were no scenes and no disorder. After a further five minutes the
    room was ventilated. Specially assigned SS people collected the dead on
    special stretchers and took them to the crematoria.[11]

Brandenburg and Grafeneck operated until late 1940. By then four
other killing centres - Hartheim, Sonnenstein, Bernburg and
Hadamar - had also been established. The killing process was similar
in all the institutions. Suitable rooms were easily converted into gas
chambers by being sealed and then having a few metres of gas pipe

laid. Different chambers could hold different numbers of people. Grafeneck at first held 40-50 but was later enlarged to hold 75. The killing technique was efficient. Most people went unsuspectingly to their deaths. Removal of the corpses' gold teeth and the cremation of the bodies took far longer than the actual killing.

After 1945 most T-4 staff claimed they feared punishment if they refused to participate. This was simply a convenient excuse. All the evidence suggests that all the staff who participated in the T-4 operations did so voluntarily. They were selected mainly through a network of personal and Party connections. They were not ordered to comply - and nothing unpleasant happened to those who refused. Nor were the T-4 managers merely 'desk-bound murderers'. Many attended experimental gassings and inspected the killing centres to see that everything was in order. Most were loyal Nazis and felt no moral qualms about what was going on. Even after the war, most T-4 managers did not accept that their deeds amounted to murder. They saw themselves as involved in humane mercy killings. The 40 or so T-4 doctors seem to have had similar motivation to the managers. Most were young and ambitious and realised that there were opportunities for rapid promotion if they co-operated. Moreover, all accepted the eugenic goals of the Nazi regime. The managers of the killing centres - often police officers, loaned from the SS - seem to have sought the jobs for professional advancement but were also aware - and proud - that they were making history. Nursing staff also willingly collaborated. Many of the other staff (for example, the 'stokers' who helped rip out the gold teeth and take the bodies to the crematoria) quickly became cynical and hard-bitten.

Great efforts were made to conceal what was going on. All the T-4 employees signed an oath of silence. The relatives or guardians of the victims were notified that they had arrived safely at their new institution, even though they were already actually dead when the notification was sent. Then, usually ten days later, the relatives were informed that the patient had died of natural causes and that the body had been cremated. If requested, relatives could be sent an urn containing the ashes of the deceased. The urns did not contain the correct ashes.

Despite all the efforts to preserve secrecy, information soon began to filter out. The deaths of so many people, so soon after arrival at a new clinic, obviously aroused suspicion - as did the smell of burning flesh. As with children's euthanasia, many relatives supported the T-4 programme if only because it rid them of the burden of paying the asylum fees. This silent collusion facilitated the euthanasia programme. Yet, not everyone turned a blind eye. Some relatives turned to the courts for guidance and redress. Since euthanasia had not been officially legalised, the courts were uncertain how to respond. Not until April 1941 did leaders of the judiciary finally receive detailed information about the euthanasia programme from Brack. Hitler's written authorisation was passed round the room for inspection. None present raised any objection.

Catholic and Protestant churches controlled many of the asylums. A few church-run institutions did try to prevent or delay the transfer of their patients, but without much success. In general, the response of church leaders, most of whom were anxious to avoid a confrontation with Hitler, was slow and hesitant. Only a few protested. The most striking on the Protestant side was Pastor Braun, who wrote a strong letter to Hitler in July 1940. A few weeks later he was arrested by the *Gestapo* (but soon released). Opposition from the Catholic Church culminated in a - mild - protest in August 1940 by the Fulda Bishops' Conference. In December 1940 the Vatican issued a statement condemning euthanasia and asserting the sanctity of human life. But the Papacy made no attempt to mobilise Catholics by a specific condemnation of the T-4 programme.

The most serious attack came in August 1941 when Bishop von Galen of Munster issued a sermon publicly denouncing the T-4 killings. Thousands of copies of his sermon were printed and circulated. The Nazi leadership was furious. But Hitler, unwilling to make Galen a martyr, refused to sanction any move against him. A few days later, Hitler, apparently fearful of alienating large numbers of Germans, ordered a stop to the gassings. The rumour was circulated that he had been unaware of the killing and that as soon as he was informed, he ordered it to stop. By then over 70,000 people had been killed.

Euthanasia did not end with Hitler's stop order in August 1941, which was simply a tactical retreat. Children's euthanasia continued without interruption until 1945. Adult euthanasia quickly resumed but out of public view. Rather than being gassed, thousands of asylum patients continued to die as a result of malnutrition and drug overdoses. Meanwhile, the gassing centres of Sonnenstein, Hartheim and Bernberg soon had other victims. In the spring of 1941, Bouhler and Himmler agreed a scheme (code named 14f13) by which concentration camp prisoners who were sick and incapable of work should be gassed. T-4 doctors visited the camps and decided who should be transferred to the gassing centres. Although the exact number will never be known, many thousands of people died as a result of the14f13 programme.

The euthanasia programme was the Nazis' first attempt at organising systematic mass murder, preceding the Holocaust by many months. By 1941 T-4 had developed efficient techniques for the murder of thousands of humans. After August 1941 many of the agents of T-4 were transferred east to deal with an even larger problem - the murder of millions of Jews.

8 Conclusion

Nazi Jewish policy from September 1939 to June 1941 *can* be seen as

Hitler deliberately marking time while waiting for the opportunity to carry out genocide in conjunction with an invasion of the USSR. The Madagascar plan *can* be seen as a device to fool world opinion. The policy of confining Jews to sealed ghettos *can* be seen as a major step toward assembling them in preparation for extermination.

However, Nazi policy does not seem to have been set on genocide in the period 1939-41. The forced emigration of all German-controlled Jews, whether to the General Government or to Madagascar, remained the 'final solution' until early 1941. The Madagascar plan was taken very seriously. German civil servants busied themselves laying the foundations for the scheme and German advisers were sent to both occupied and friendly countries to prepare them for the great evacuation. The fact that leading Nazis spoke of the coming deportation as the 'final solution' once confused historians. Some cited it as proof of the existence of an extermination plan. But it is now clear that in 1940 the term simply meant clearing Europe of Jews by deportation.

Hitler's speeches and actions give no indication of any extermination plans in 1939-40. Indeed, he spoke of the Jews as 'stupid adversaries' who had proved to be far less powerful than he had feared. Hitler's main lieutenants took their lead from him. After talks with Hitler on two occasions (November 1940 and March 1941) Goebbels noted in his diary that the Jews would be deported from Europe. Himmler in 1940 regarded extermination as 'impossible' and 'contrary to the German nature'. If Himmler was not thinking of extermination, it is unlikely that anyone else was. Hitler and Himmler had a close and sympathetic relationship in the formulation and implementation of racial policy. In Browning's view, 'If one wants to know what Hitler was thinking, one should look at what Himmler was doing.'[12] In 1939-40 Himmler was deeply involved in a massive (but hastily improvised) plan to racially restructure much of eastern Europe. Nazi Jewish policy in Poland was simply part of this demographic project and did not yet have priority within it. The resettlement of ethnic Germans from the USSR and the Baltic States was the centrepiece of Nazi racial policy. Polish peasants (rather than urban Jews) were more likely to be moved to the General Government to accommodate the incoming Germans. Attempts to set in motion full-scale Jewish deportation in 1939-40 all came to nothing.

If Hitler was thinking in terms of the mass slaughter of all European Jewry in the years 1939-41, why were German Jews still encouraged to emigrate? (Some 70,000 did so.) Why were the Polish Jews not systematically killed? If Hitler could order the killing of 70,000 Germans through the euthanasia programme, why was the time not opportune to murder the Jews?

However, the fact that Nazi Jewish policy continued to be evolutionary, not programmatic, in itself posed a potential threat to Jews. According to Browning, Hitler's anti-Jewish policies tended to fluctuate with his moods. In September 1939, in the euphoria of victory over Poland, he approved plans for a demographic re-organisation of eastern Europe. In June 1940, with victory over France, he approved the Madagascar plan. More victories might lead to more radical policies. Moreover, those Nazis who had to cope with the Jewish question were, by 1941, becoming seriously frustrated. Hitler continuously emphasised his determination to rid Europe of Jews. None of his lieutenants could afford to ignore this. Thus they continuously raised the subject with Hitler, zealously hammering home to him the increasingly burdensome absence of a solution to the Jewish problem. The pressure was thus a two-way process. By 1941 some Nazis felt that a more brutal final solution was necessary. The Jews in the Polish ghettos were (as a result of Nazi policy) living like animals. Some (like Goebbels) argued they should be treated like animals and put down.

It was Hitler, however, not Goebbels who decided Jewish policy. What did he intend? It is worth remembering that Hitler had showed no mercy to the Polish elite, or to the Jews in the Polish ghettos and labour camps, or to mentally and physically handicapped Germans. T-4 was very much a laboratory for mass murder. If Hitler did secretly harbour the intention of destroying Jews, rather than merely expelling them, the apparatus of destruction was taking shape. The executioners were trained, the technology proved, the procedures worked out. Hitler had been prepared to issue orders for mass euthanasia. Given that he regarded the Jews as more dangerous than the German handicapped, he was unlikely to find it hard to give a genocidal order. Hitler increasingly saw himself as a man of destiny. By 1941 his prestige was at its peak. He could do as he wished in Germany and indeed in most of Europe. Perhaps, as Browning has pointed out, the euphoria of further victory might tempt 'an elated Hitler to dare even more drastic policies'.[13]

References
1   J. Noakes and G. Pridham (eds), *Nazism: 1919-1945*, vol 3 (University of Exeter 1987), p. 930.
2   Ibid, p. 939-40.
3   Ibid, p. 933.
4   Ibid, p. 1053.
5   Ibid, p. 1063.
6   Ibid, p. 1067-9.
7   Ibid, p. 1070.
8   Christopher R. Browning, *The Path to Genocide* (Cambridge University Press, 1992), p.30.
9   J. Noakes and G. Pridham (eds), *Nazism*, vol 3, p. 1005.
10 Ibid, p. 1013.
11 Ibid, p. 1019-20.
12 Browning, *Path to Genocide*, p. 121.
13 Ibid.

Summary Diagram
The Effect of War: 1939-41

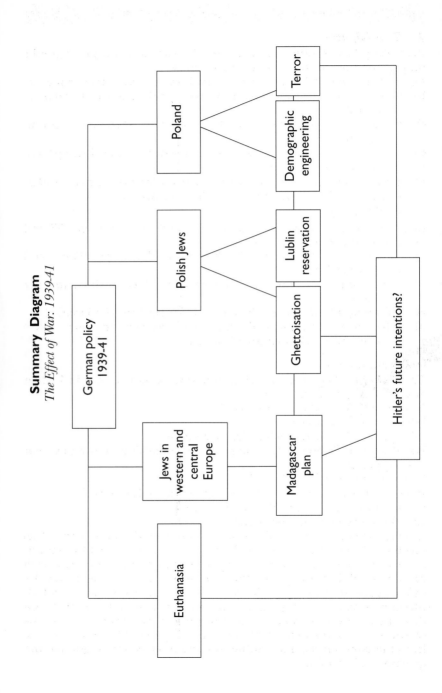

Source-based questions on 'The Effects of War: 1939-41'

1. The Ghettos

Read Rozycki's account and examine the statistics and photographs on page 64. Answer the following questions:

a) To what extent do the sources corroborate each other? (8 marks)
b) Comment on the validity and reliability of the statistical evidence. (5 marks)
c) Comment on the validity and reliability of Rozycki's account. (5 marks)
d) Comment on the validity and reliability of Heinrich Jost's photographic evidence. (5 marks)
e) What other types of sources might exist to help historians understand what life in the ghettos was like? (7 marks)

2. Euthanasia

Read the extracts from Hefelmann and Dr Becker on pages 67 and 69. Answer the following questions:

a) Which of the two sources is likely to be the more reliable and why? (5 marks)
b) Which of the two sources is likely to be the less reliable and why? (5 marks)
c) How might both sources be checked for reliability? (5 marks)
d) What, if any, relevance do these sources have for our understanding of the Holocaust? (5 marks)

Hints and Advice

The following key questions should always be borne in mind when answering source-based questions:

Is the source what it purports to be?
When was it produced?
Who produced it and in what circumstances?
Was the person who created the source well positioned to know what was happening?
Why was the source produced?
What was the intended or expected audience of the source?
In what way is the source affected by bias?
Can the source be corroborated?

Sometimes a source is obviously coloured by the prejudices of its producer. But don't necessarily discount it on that score. Most - if not all - sources are biased in some way. Even those that are most biased can be useful. If nothing else, they can display the attitude of individuals or groups at the time. More important than the bias might be whether a source's originator was badly 'positioned' to 'see' and describe an event. Remember that historians ask different questions of sources and thus can sometimes obtain very different evidence from the same source. Put another way: a source is only as good as the questions asked of it.

Let's now turn to question 1.

a) Historians are always happiest when sources corroborate each other. Do these sources tend to agree? To what extent, if any, do they disagree? Are they all from the same time?

b) It is often said that 'there are lies, damned lies and statistics'. Who do you think compiled these statistics and why? Can you be sure the statistics are accurate?

c) Why do you think Rozycki wrote a long account of the situation in the Warsaw ghetto? (You have only a part of his account.) What was his bias? Does this make the source more or less reliable?

d) It is essential not to rush the analysis of visual sources. While it takes time to read written sources, it is possible to take in illustrations at a glance. It is thus easy to form conclusions too quickly. It is good advice, therefore, to make a conscious effort to go slowly when analysing visual material. Photographs (like paintings and cartoons) invariably contain more than we imagine, so scrutinise each illustration carefully and thoroughly. Remember that photographs can sometimes lie! Why do you think Jost (a German army sergeant) took the photographs? Does this affect the validity and reliability of his photographic evidence?

e) Use your imagination! There are plenty of types of sources available to twentieth-century historians: indeed, often far too many types and far too many sources. Which sources would be essential in giving us a balanced view of life in the Warsaw ghetto?

You are on your own for question 2!

5 The Final Solution: 1941-5

1 Introduction

On 22 June 1941 Hitler launched Operation Barbarossa - the attack on the USSR. He was now fighting the war he had always wanted. Victory, as well as giving him control of all Europe, would provide the opportunity to destroy 'Jewish Bolshevism' and win *lebensraum* for the German master race. Defeat, on the other hand, would mean disaster. Given the colossal stakes involved, the war against the USSR was to be different in kind from the war in the west: it was to be a brutal and uncompromising war to the death. At first everything went well for Hitler. His forces won a series of major battles, capturing millions of prisoners and occupying huge swathes of land. As German troops penetrated deeper into Russia, special units of police and SS waged an unprecedented campaign of murder against Communist officials and Jews. This was the prelude to the Holocaust - the systematic extermination of all European Jews. A great deal of controversy surrounds this 'Final Solution', not least the question of when, but also the process by which, the genocide decision was made.

2 Operation Barbarossa

American historian Richard Breitman has recently claimed that Hitler made the fateful decision to exterminate all European Jews not later than January 1941, as the planning for Operation Barbarossa went ahead: the Final Solution thereafter just became a matter of 'time and timing'.[1] However, Breitman has provided little but circumstantial evidence to support his case. Given the lack of hard evidence, most Holocaust historians think that the genocide decision came later. Yet there is absolutely no doubt that Hitler was determined to defeat and destroy 'Jewish-Bolshevists'.

On 3 March 1941 he issued a secret directive to his army high command insisting that 'the Bolshevik/Jewish intelligentsia' in the USSR 'must be eliminated', in the same way that the Polish elite had been annihilated. While some army leaders had opposed the massacre of Polish civilians, all seem to have accepted Hitler's call for unprecedented brutality in the USSR. In part, this reflected the army's increased faith in Hitler after the military successes of 1939-41. In part, it reflected the fact that most German officers shared Hitler's hatred of Bolshevism and Judaism (which they saw as one and the same) and his belief that the demonised enemy had to be beaten, whatever the cost. In early March the army high command accepted that the SS should be entrusted with 'special tasks' in the conquered areas of the USSR, and that Himmler should have special independent powers. Army directives, issued on 19 May, proclaimed that the war against the USSR would require 'ruthless and energetic action against Bolshevik agitators, guerrillas, saboteurs, and Jews, and the total elimination of all active or passive resistance'.[2] On 6 June 1941, army leaders ordered that political commissars (Communist Party officials), 'the initiators of barbaric, asiatic methods of combat', were to be shot after being taken prisoner.

Army leaders, while accepting the need for brutal measures, were happy to leave implementation of most of the dirty work to the SS and to the *Einsatzgruppen*. In June 1941 there were four *Einsatzgruppen* - A to D - attached to the four army groups that would invade the USSR. Each *Einsatzgruppen*, roughly 1,000 men strong, was divided into smaller units called *Einsatzkommandos*. Most men in the *Einsatzgruppen* were ordinary policemen, hurriedly seconded from various police departments. The officers, on the other hand, were carefully selected. Well-educated, ambitious, and successful, they were committed Nazis. Otto Ohlendorf, commander of *Einsatzgruppen D*, was typical. A tall, handsome 34-year-old lawyer, he held degrees in both economics and law.

Although the commanders had been briefed by Heydrich in Berlin (on 17 June 1941) and knew in general terms what was expected of them, the precise content of their orders is a matter of controversy. After 1945 surviving *Einsatzgruppen* leaders gave conflicting evidence about the orders they had received. At the Nuremberg trials, Ohlendorf and several other *Einsatzkommando* leaders, testified that an order to kill all the Jews had been given shortly before the start of the campaign by Bruno Streckenbach, chief of the personnel for the Reich Main Security Office (RSHA), on instructions from Himmler. However, other *Einsatzgruppen* leaders later testified that they had received no such order until some time in August or September 1941. Furthermore Streckenbach, who was thought to be dead in 1945, emerged from a Soviet prison camp in the mid-1950s and denied having given the order. Three of the Nuremberg defendants then retracted their statements, saying that they had been made in an attempt to save Ohlendorf from the gallows.

To further complicate matters, it seems that different *Einsatzgruppen* did slightly different things at slightly different times in the summer of 1941. Generally, after entering Russian towns, they rounded up and shot Communist leaders and Jews. In some areas, especially the Baltic States and the Ukraine, where anti-Semitism was deep-rooted and where Jews were seen as representatives of the USSR, the *Einsatzgruppen* were helped by the local populace who enthusiastically joined in pogrom-style killings. After a year under Soviet rule, many people in the Baltic States had their own scores to settle. Some Ukrainians had the scores of many years to settle.

The *Einsatzgruppen* leaders had certainly been given the task of liquidating potential enemies. However, by no means all Jewish men and relatively few Jewish women and children were killed in

June/July. This very much suggests that there was no pre-invasion genocide order. Swiss historian Philippe Burrin has also pointed out that 4,000 policemen, not specially trained in mass killing techniques, were hardly likely to be thought sufficient to kill five million Russian Jews. While most historians accept that the extensive shootings of Jews in June/July marked a 'quantum leap'[3] in the direction of genocide, there is a world of difference between savage violence and cold-blooded, systematic genocide. In the first weeks of Operation Barbarossa, Soviet commissars were more likely to be shot than ordinary Jews. Moreover some of the first (and worst) outrages against Jews were committed not by the *Einsatzgruppen* but by local people.

On 2 July Heydrich issued written instructions to the *Einsatzgruppen* commanders. Leading Communist officials, 'Jews in the service of the Party or the State' and other extremist elements were to be executed and pogroms by local people should be 'encouraged'. On 17 July Heydrich issued an order that all Jews among Russian prisoners of war were to be executed by the SS. While neither of these directives is proof of the existence of a genocide order, both show that Nazi attitudes were hardening. Nevertheless, Alfred Rosenberg, head of the occupied Soviet territory (the Eastern Territories), was still not preparing for genocide. For Rosenberg, the final solution was still the resettlement of the Jews in indeterminate territory somewhere in the east. If an extermination programme for Soviet Jewry existed, he seems to have known nothing about it. It seems unlikely that Hitler would not have informed Rosenberg of a decision of such magnitude and of such vital concern to him. There is also evidence that not even Himmler was preparing for genocide. A July 1941 plan suggests that, while he expected a brief period of killing, he then envisaged massive population movement. Over a 30-year period, some 31 million people from the Eastern Territories were to be expelled to Siberia and replaced by 4.5 million Germans. The deportees would include Soviet Jews. This does not suggest that the Holocaust had yet been planned. The final evidence is statistical. Up until mid-August 1941, about 50,000 Soviet Jews are thought to have been killed: this was a modest figure given that 500,000 were to be killed in the next four months.

Browning thinks that an elated Hitler, confident that victory over the USSR was at hand, gave signals to carry out 'racial cleansing' in mid-July 1941. Apparently master of all of Europe, he no longer had to worry about world opinion. Interestingly, both Himmler and Heydrich were in close proximity to his headquarters from 15-20 July. Here was an opportunity for Hitler to have confided new orders. Certainly events now began to gather momentum. In late July Hitler committed two SS brigades (over 11,000 men) to assist the overburdened *Einsatzgruppen*. This was only the start of the build-up. By the end of 1941 there were some 60,000 men in *Einsatzgruppen* or police battalions on Soviet territory - sufficient manpower to kill on a massive scale.

In August 1941 Himmler travelled through much of the Eastern Territories and was thus in a position to confirm the new policy. The fact that he issued personal instructions probably explains why different *Einsatzgruppen* leaders learned of the new turn in policy at different times. Whatever the precise time-scale, there is no doubt that by late August the killing of Jews was on a different scale. Jewish women and children were now routinely massacred. In June/July most of the victims were shot individually by firing squad. By August, however, hundreds at a time were forced to lie in or kneel at the edge of a trench (which they had often dug themselves) before being shot in the back of the head.

3 The Final Solution: the Decision

By September 1941 the mass slaughter of Russian Jews was well underway. However, what Hitler had in store for Jews in other parts of Europe remains unclear. Browning is convinced that Hitler was considering killing all Jews in July 1941 and asked Himmler and Heydrich to come up with a genocide 'feasibility study': after all, it was illogical to kill Russian Jews and then transport Polish Jews into the vacuum thus created. In Browning's view, the mass murder of Jews was the first use to which German victory was going to be put: 'in the euphoria of seeming victory [in July 1941] Hitler solicited a plan to extend the killing process already underway in Russia to the rest of Europe's Jews'.[4]

On 31 July Goering sent the following document to Heydrich:

1 I hereby charge you with making all necessary preparations with regard to organisational, technical and material matters for bringing about a complete solution of the Jewish question within the German sphere of influence in Europe. ... I request you further to send me, in the near
5 future, an overall plan covering the organisational, technical and material measures necessary for the accomplishment of the final solution of the Jewish question which we desire.[5]

Goering did not initiate but only signed this authorisation, which was actually prepared by Heydrich's office. (Heydrich was thus essentially giving orders to himself!) Nevertheless, historian Raul Hilberg regards the Goering document as a critical 'turning point'. Browning agrees. Given that the SS already had far-reaching authority, Heydrich did not need Goering's authorisation to continue expulsion/extermination activities. The 31 July document thus suggests that Heydrich now knew he faced a new and awesome task that dwarfed even the *Einsatzgruppen* massacres.

However, other historians are not convinced. Some think the 31 July document simply represented an extension of Heydrich's responsibility for the Jewish question beyond Germany's borders. They point out that neither Heydrich nor Goering, in fact, behaved in the days following 31 July as if the decision to kill all Europe's Jews had been taken. There are no signs in August of frenzied activity to organise a genocide programme.

Historians like Burrin and Kershaw are not convinced that the surge of killings in the USSR meant that Hitler had yet decided to kill all of Europe's Jews. They think that Hitler's decision came later - either in September or October 1941 - and had little to do with the euphoria of victory. 'Everything seems to suggest that there was a decision-making process lasting several weeks before the fatal verdict was handed down in September', thinks Burrin.[6] Kershaw stresses that 'unequivocal signs of actual planning of systematic genocide in Poland, the key area, are not to be found before October'.[7] Burrin and Kershaw believe that Hitler finally decided on genocide more out of a sense of desperation than of elation. By September 1941 Operation Barbarossa was not going to plan. The campaign, which the Germans had anticipated would last no more than four months, was far from over. By August, Hitler was increasingly anxious. The longer the USSR kept up the fight, the greater the danger of guerrilla war. Thus there was a need for even harsher methods to keep the occupied areas under control. Moreover, German casualties continued to mount. According to Burrin, Hitler decided that the Jews would have to foot the bill for the spilling of so much German blood. The central decision in late September or early October, claims Burrin, 'had arisen from a murderous rage increasingly exacerbated by the ordeal of the failure of his campaign in Russia'.[8] By killing his archetypal enemies, he was demonstrating his will to fight to the end.

It is, of course, possible that Hitler gave two extermination orders: one concerning Russian Jews in July 1941 and another later in 1941 affecting the rest of European Jewry. This is Browning's view. Having ordered the killing of Russian Jews and the setting up of a feasibility study, Browning believes that Hitler vacillated between July and September - his mood fluctuating as the fortunes of war in the USSR fluctuated. From mid-September 1941 until mid-October 1941, however, the fighting suddenly swung in Germany's favour. At some stage in September/October 1941, with the second peak of German military success, Browning thinks Hitler unleashed the second great intensification of the Holocaust.

Given that documentation is scarce and that most of the chief people responsible for the Holocaust died before the end of the war, the debate about the precise timing of the Final Solution looks set to continue. But most Holocaust historians now accept Burrin's view that the pieces of the Holocaust fell into place between 18 September and 18 October 1941. The vast majority also believe that it was Hitler who initiated the Holocaust. Nothing so radical could have begun without his approval. Admittedly the factors which led to his decision remain speculative, but events do seem to have been propelling him towards a violent solution to the Jewish problem. The slaughter of Soviet Jews would enable Hitler to break out of the vicious circle in which military success brought millions more Jews under German control. Once he resolved to kill all Russian Jews it was but a small step to decide to kill all Jews. Just as with the euthanasia programme, Hitler seems to have been anxious to avoid associating himself too closely with the Holocaust. Thus he probably left it to Goering and Himmler to sort matters out between themselves, having given them the go-ahead in general terms. It is possible that Hitler authorised Himmler to produce a solution to the Jewish question without enquiring too closely into what would be involved. But since any genocide solution required the involvement of numerous state agencies, some form of authorisation from Hitler was necessary. At no stage were local officials acting on their own initiative. They were obeying orders from Himmler, who in turn was obeying Hitler's orders. Himmler later said: 'I do nothing that the Führer does not know.'

4 The Final Solution in the USSR

By mid-August 1941 all the *Einsatzgruppen* interpreted their task as the extermination of all Soviet Jews. Karl Jager, head of *Einsatzkommando 3* of *Einsatzgruppen A*, kept extensive execution records. In July 1941, the *kommando* killed 4,293 Jews, of whom only 135 were women. In September 1941, by contrast, the *kommando* killed 56,459 Jews - 15,104 men, 26,243 women and 15,112 children. By 25 November Jager reported the following number of deaths: 1,064 Communists, 56 partisans, 653 mentally ill, 44 Poles, 28 Russian prisoners, 5 Gypsies, 1 Armenian, and 136,421 Jews. The situation was the same elsewhere. Perhaps the most notorious killing took place outside Kiev (the USSR's third largest city) in September 1941. A few days after the capture of the town on 19 September 1941 a huge explosion killed many German soldiers in the Continental Hotel, the German army headquarters. In reprisal, 33,771 Jews were shot, over a three-day period, at the Babi Yar ravine on the outskirts of Kiev.

Not only the *Einsatzgruppen* carried out the killings. Auxiliary forces, recruited from people of the Baltic States and the Ukraine, were also willing executioners. So were ordinary German soldiers. The mass shootings of Jews had the support of the army authorities. The following order was issued by Field-Marshal von Reichenau on 10 October 1941:

1   The main aim of the campaign against the Jewish-Bolshevist system is the complete destruction of its forces and the extermination of the asiatic influence on the sphere of European culture. As a result, the troops have to take on tasks which go beyond the conventional purely
5   military ones. In the eastern sphere the soldier is not simply a fighter

according to the rules of war, but the supporter of a ruthless racial ideology and the avenger of all the bestialities which have been inflicted on the German nation and those ethnic groups related to it. For this reason soldiers must show full understanding for the necessity for the
10 severe but just atonement required of the Jewish subhumans. It also has the further purpose of nipping in the bud uprisings in the rear of the *Wehrmacht* which experience shows are invariably instigated by Jews.[9]

On 28 October, after Hitler described Reichenau's order as excellent, the army high command instructed all its field commanders to issue orders along the same lines.

After 1945 the *Wehrmacht* tried to hide the fact that it was involved in the Holocaust. However, there is now little doubt about its complicity in the USSR killings - at every level. Army leaders gave the commands and ordinary soldiers willingly carried them out. Indeed they sometimes undertook brutal 'cleansing' operations on their own initiative. The 'primeval'[10] fighting on the eastern front in the Second World War seems to have had a particularly brutalising effect on German troops. The nature of the war - the terrible climatic conditions, the horrendous losses (the Germans suffered some six million casualties in the USSR), the cultural differences between the invaders and the occupied - resulted in German soldiers becoming indifferent to death and suffering. The murder of tens of thousands of Jews was viewed by many as an unavoidable by-product of the battle for survival: probably few had serious misgivings about it. The German army was thus a crucial part of the genocidal machinery in the USSR.

The following description of a killing in the Ukraine in 1942 was given by Hermann Graebe, a German engineer, to a Nuremberg tribunal in 1945.

1 The people who had got off the lorries - men, women, and children of all ages - had to undress on the orders of an SS man who was carrying a riding or dog whip in his hand. ... Without weeping or crying out these people undressed and stood together in family groups, embracing
5 each other and saying good-bye while waiting for a sign from another SS man who stood on the edge of the ditch and who also had a whip. During the 15 minutes which I stood near the ditch, I did not hear a single complaint or a plea for mercy. I watched a family of about eight, a man and a woman, both about fifty years old with their children of
10 about one, eight, and ten, as well as two grown-up daughters of about twenty and twenty-four. An old woman with snow-white hair held a one-year-old child in her arms singing to it and tickling it. The child squeaked with delight. The married couple looked on with tears in their eyes. The father held the ten-year-old boy by the hand speaking softly to
15 him. The boy was struggling to hold back the tears. The father pointed a finger to the sky and stroked his head and seemed to be explaining something to him. At this moment, the SS man near the ditch called out

something to his comrade. The latter counted off about twenty people,
and ordered them behind the mound. The family of which I have just
20 spoken was among them. ... I walked round the mound and stood in
front of the huge grave. The bodies were lying so tightly packed together
that only their heads showed, from almost all of which blood ran down
over their shoulders. Some were still moving. Others raised their hands
and turned their heads to show they were still alive. The ditch was
25 already three quarters full. I estimate that it already held about a thousand bodies. I turned my eyes towards the man doing the shooting. He
was an SS man; he sat, legs swinging, on the edge of the ditch. He had an
automatic rifle resting on his knees and was smoking a cigarette. The
people, completely naked, climbed down steps which had been cut into
30 the clay wall of the ditch, stumbled over the heads of those lying there
and stopped at the spot indicated by the SS man. They lay down on top
of the dead or wounded; some stroking those still living and spoke
quietly to them. Then I heard a series of rifle shots. I looked into the
ditch and saw the bodies contorting or, the heads already inert, sinking
35 on the corpses beneath.[11]

The following extract was written in January 1942 by Dr Rudolf
Lange, responsible for *Einsatzgruppen* operations in Latvia:

1 The aim of *Einsaztkommando 2* from the start was a radical solution of
the Jewish problem through the execution of all Jews. For this purpose
comprehensive purges were carried out in the whole area of our operations by special teams with the help of selected forces from the Latvian
5 auxiliary police (mainly relatives of Latvians who had been abducted or
murdered by the Bolsheviks). In early October, the number of Jews
executed in the *kommando's* sphere of operations was about 30,000. In
addition, a few thousand Jews have been eliminated by Latvian self-
defence formations off their own bat after they had been given suitable
10 encouragement. ...

It was impossible to achieve the complete elimination of Jews from
Latvia in view of the economic factors and, in particular, the demands of
the army.[12]

As the above source makes clear, economic concerns resulted in
some Jews escaping immediate death. This issue produced considerable friction between civilian authorities and the army on the one
hand, and the SS on the other. Orders from Berlin in December
1941 made it clear that 'economic considerations are to be regarded
as fundamentally irrelevant in the settlement of the problem'.
However, in practice, a compromise was struck between the SS and
the army and economic agencies, whereby a few Jews were given a
stay of execution for labour purposes. Nevertheless, over the next
two years the Russian ghettos were progressively liquidated, first
through piecemeal selections of those no longer capable of work,
and then, more comprehensively, during the so-called 'second

Einsatzkommandos *force Jewish women from the village of Misocz in the Ukraine*

The women's corpses after the execution. Two of the German execution squad kill the victims who survived the initial shooting

sweep' starting in the summer of 1942.

The numbers of Jews killed in the course of the *Einsatzgruppen* operations in the USSR can only be estimated. During the first sweep from June 1941 to April 1942 some 750,000 were probably murdered. A further 1.5 million may have been killed in the second sweep of 1942-3. Most of the victims were shot - sometimes by machine gun. A number died in special gas vans, used from December 1941. Others died in labour camps where they were worked to death or succumbed to disease brought about by malnutrition.

It was not just Jews who suffered. The fate of the non-Jewish peoples in the occupied zones depended essentially on the Nazis' conception of where they came on the racial scale. The Estonians, Latvians and Lithuanians, who were considered partially German, were treated reasonably well. Other peoples were not so fortunate. The 40 million Ukrainians, whose hatred for Soviet oppression was so intense that most welcomed the Germans at first, were soon in the grip of a terror similar to that in Poland. Disobedience of the most trivial kind resulted in summary execution. Tens of thousands of able-bodied Ukrainians were transported to Germany as slave labourers.

5 The Fate of the German Jews

From August 1941 it became illegal for German Jews to emigrate voluntarily. On 1 September all Jews were forced to wear the yellow star of David sewn on their clothing, a move which facilitated the implementation of further anti-Semitic measures. Later that month Hitler declared that the Reich should be liberated of Jews 'as rapidly as possible'. In October Eichmann began transporting German Jews eastwards. Given the situation in Germany, it was not too difficult to find volunteers. Those Jews who were to be 'resettled' in the east were allowed to take with them some money, a case or two of luggage and food for the journey. (The rest of their property was confiscated by the state.) Whatever feelings of optimism the 20,000 Jews who were deported to Lodz in October 1941 had ended as soon as they reached their destination. Some of those deemed incapable of working were killed on arrival. The rest were dumped in the over-crowded ghetto, where many died from starvation and disease. Protests from the authorities in Warthegau about their inability to absorb more Jews led to a temporary end of the transportations to Lodz on 4 November. By then there were other - worse - destinations.

In November and December 1941 some 25,000 Reich Jews were deported to Riga, Minsk and Kovno, towns in the Ostland - a territory in which the *Einsatzgruppen* operated. (See map on page 26.) Events in Ostland suggest that, if the ultimate fate of Jews was not in doubt, the actual timing and form of killing was largely improvised, with members of each transport having different experiences depending on where and when they arrived. Some Jews were spared to eke out a survival in the ghettos or nearby labour camps. But in late November 1941, five transports of Jews were massacred at Kovno soon after their arrival and without prior screening to select those fit for labour. The same thing happened in Riga on 30 November 1941. 14,000 Jews from Riga itself were massacred, as well as 1,000 Jews who had arrived from Berlin the night before. On 8 December another 13,000 were massacred on the outskirts of Riga. After the war the Ostland SS police leader claimed that Himmler had told him (in November) that 'all Jews in the Ostland must be exterminated right down to the very last one'. Even so, it seems to have been presumed that there would be a Jewish presence for some time in both Riga and Minsk. Trains of Jewish deportees continued to arrive in both towns until the spring of 1942.

6 The Start of Gassing

Until the winter of 1941-2 the main method of eliminating Jews was mass shootings. While effective in terms of the number killed, this method had some disadvantages, not least the fact that such massacres were hard to conceal, as well as occasionally producing psychological stress among the killers. In August 1941 Himmler commissioned his SS technical advisers to test different ways of killing and recommend those which were more efficient and more 'humane'. Tests with explosives proved to be a gruesome failure. Not surprisingly the SS soon hit upon the idea of gas, which had proved to be a highly effective method in the euthanasia programme. Added to this was the fact that Hitler's Chancellery was eager to redeploy the T-4 personnel.

The initial gassing experiment occurred in the Warthegau. By the autumn of 1941 conditions in the Lodz ghetto were appalling and thousands more Jews were still expected. In October Wilhelm Koppe, the area's police chief, aware of the thinking in Berlin, appointed Herbert Lange to find a suitable place for the killing of Warthegau's Jews. (Koppe had already used a special unit commanded by Lange in 1940 to kill some 1,500 mental patients.) In early November Lange recommended Chelmno, some 40 miles north-west of Lodz. An SS team set about converting an old mansion into a barracks where Jews would arrive and undress. A forest clearing, some three miles from the village, was chosen as the site for a mass grave. The first victims in December 1941 were killed in gas vans, the exhaust fumes from which were taken by pipes into the sealed rear. By January 1942 a permanent gas chamber was in use. Chelmno was a pure killing centre: it had no labour camp. By the time it was destroyed in March 1943, some 140,000 Jews (and a few thousand Gypsies, Poles and Russians) are thought to have died there.

Himmler selected Odilo Globocnik, the Lublin police chief, to oversee the killing of Jews in the General Government. Dozens of SS and ex-T-4 men were assigned to him in the autumn of 1941. His task was to construct and run a number of death camps in the Lublin region. Work at Belzec, the first of three sites, began in November 1941. Meanwhile, at Auschwitz (in Upper Silesia), the first gassing experiments on Russian prisoners of war took place in September 1941.

7 The Wannsee Conference

Having launched the deportation process in Germany in October 1941, the RSHA soon found itself facing a number of practical problems. Careful co-ordination of various agencies - police, finance, and railway departments - both within Germany and in the occupied countries, was required if thousands of Jews were to be transported to Poland. Accordingly in November 1941 Heydrich invited senior officials from several agencies to discuss logistical and other matters. The Wannsee Conference, initially planned for December 1941, was finally held on 20 January 1942. Most of the representatives were top civil servants: 7 of the 15 participants held doctoral degrees. The meeting, chaired by Heydrich and lasting only 90 minutes, formulated common procedures whereby all of Europe's 11 million Jews were to be rounded up and 'resettled' in the east. The Conference also established the principle that those who were considered fit should be given temporary reprieve and set to work (effectively to death) in labour gangs. The fate of the unfit was not discussed directly, but the implication was clear: they were to be massacred straight away. The Conference minutes, prepared by Eichmann and edited by Heydrich, had a relatively wide circulation and did not therefore spell out extermination: instead they used terms like 'legalised removal' and 'resettlement'. However, those attending the Conference certainly realised that 'resettlement' meant extermination, one way or another. At his trial in 1960, Eichmann was rather franker about the Conference than he was in the minutes: 'the gentlemen ... talked about the matter without mincing their words. ... The talk was of killing, elimination and liquidation.'[13]

The significance of the Wannsee Conference was not that it was the starting point of the Final Solution: that was already underway. It was, however, the moment when it was endorsed by a broad segment of the German government (and not just the SS). The Conference also helped dot the 'i's and cross the 't's of procedures, ensuring that by the spring of 1942 the extermination programme was turned into a quasi-industrial process for the efficient destruction of human beings.

Interestingly the Wannsee Conference (and further conferences on this matter) failed to agree on the status and treatment of the *Mischlinge* (the half-Jews), with the result that most *Mischlinge* were not deported. Hitler probably did not think pursuing the matter was worth the discontent it would cause among the Aryan relatives of those involved.

8 Operation Reinhard

The mass gassing of the Jews in the General Government (which gathered momentum in 1942) is usually known as Operation Reinhard - after Reinhard Heydrich (who was assassinated by Czech partisans in May 1942). Belzec was the first functional Operation Reinhard camp (see map on page 26, in Chapter 2, for the location of the killing centres). The camp commandant, Christian Wirth, and several of his staff had previous T-4 experience. Constructed in a remote forest, Belzec was linked by a railway line to the Jewish ghetto at Lublin, 75 miles to the north. The 162-acre camp, enclosed by barbed wire, was divided into two parts. Camp 1 contained a reception area with two barracks - one for undressing and the other for storing clothes and luggage. Camp 2 contained the three small gas chambers, all in one building. A path - known as the 'tube' - 2 metres wide and 57 metres long, bordered on both sides by a wire fence, linked the two camps. Wirth tested his equipment successfully in February 1942 on several hundred Jews, and Belzec opened officially in March. Sobibor, a 100 miles to the north and an enlarged version of Belzec, started operations in May 1942. Franz Stangl, who had served at the Hartheim euthanasia centre, was appointed camp commandant. In July 1942 Stangl moved on to command the even larger camp at Treblinka, 75 miles north-east of Warsaw. Each camp had a guard contingent of about 100 Ukrainians. But the main staff consisted of about 30 SS men, most of whom were T-4 veterans.

While responsibility for clearing the ghettos and for organising the transportation to the death camps lay with the SS, the Jewish councils had the job of finding people for 're-settlement'. (Warsaw had to supply 10,000 a day from July 1942.) At first many Polish Jews, accepting the German promise of a better life in the Ukraine, were reasonably happy to be transported. But once rumours of the fate that awaited the deportees filtered back to Warsaw and elsewhere, securing volunteers became much harder. Nevertheless, thousands of Jews were daily rounded up (mainly by Jewish police) for transportation. The transportation experience was horrific. Families were usually separated and as many as 150 people crammed into closed freight cars, without food, water or toilet facilities. Sometimes hundreds died en route - suffocated, dehydrated or trampled to death. Anyone trying to escape from the trains was shot. On a typical day, transports carrying as many as 25,000 Jews made their way to the death camps.

Once the transports arrived at Belzec, Sobibor or Treblinka, the camp authorities aimed to kill all but a few of the deportees within two hours. As soon as the trains stopped, the deportees were hurried out by shouting guards. The deportees, save a few selected to serve as work-Jews, were then quickly marched to Camp 1. Here they were usually given a welcoming speech, reassuring them that they had arrived at a transit camp, from which they would be sent to the

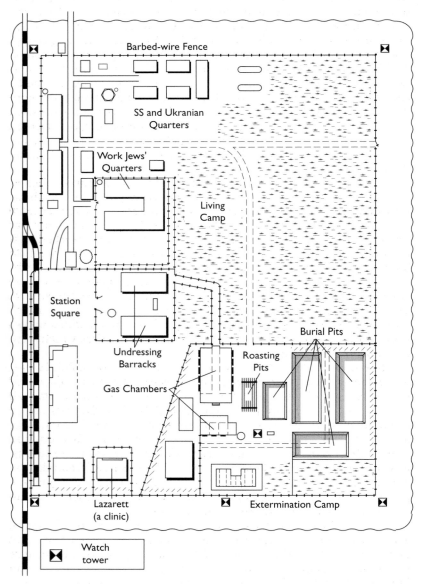

Barbed-wire Fence

SS and Ukranian
Quarters

Work Jews'
Quarters

Living
Camp

Station
Square

Undressing
Barracks

Gas Chambers

Roasting
Pits

Burial Pits

Lazarett
(a clinic)

Extermination Camp

Watch
tower

A plan of Treblinka concentration camp

Ukraine. Males and females were then separated and herded into barracks to undress. Women and girls had their hair shorn, supposedly to stop the spread of head lice. (In reality, the hair was used for several purposes, including making socks for U-boat crews.) Then, the victims (usually the men first) were forced to run down the 'tube', urged on by guards wielding whips and clubs, to the building signed 'Baths and Inhalation Rooms'. (The entrance to the 'bathhouse' at Treblinka was flanked by pots of geraniums.) The victims were now pushed into tiled chambers with fake shower nozzles. At Treblinka each chamber measured about 3.6 by 8.2 metres and could hold more than 400 victims. Once the room was full, the heavy door was closed and a diesel engine pumped in carbon monoxide gas. After 30 minutes, the engine was switched off, the doors opened, and the Jewish 'death brigade' (or *Sonderkommando*) had the job of clearing the chambers.

Initially, the bodies were dumped in enormous burial ditches. However, the burial process soon proved inadequate. At Treblinka, for example, between 23 July 1942 and 28 August 1942 some 268,000 Jews are thought to have been gassed. (Stangl testified after the war that the camp could kill 1,000 people per hour and often worked a 12-hour day.) In consequence, corpses were soon stacked everywhere. At Sobibor and Belzec, difficulties developed after burial. Swollen by heat and putrefaction, the bodies in the mass graves heaved so violently that they split the ground, creating a terrible stench. Eventually the camp authorities found that cremation was a much more efficient method of disposing of the dead. At Treblinka bodies were placed on steel girders over enormous open fires which were kept burning permanently.

While most of the victims of Operation Reinhard were Polish Jews, Jews from Germany and western Europe were sometimes transported to the three death camps. The systematic round up of Jews began all over the German empire in the spring of 1942. Told they were to be resettled in the east, Jews from western and central Europe were allowed to take some of their personal belongings with them and often travelled in proper railway cars. (Their journey, while longer, was thus less harrowing than that of Polish Jews.) At Treblinka the authorities created a fake train station to maintain the fiction that the place was merely a transit camp. Large signs indicated such non-existent amenities as a restaurant and ticket office.

Although the Operation Reinhard camps were simply death camps, a semi-permanent Jewish work force of as many as 1,000 inmates was employed in the various stages of the killing process. There were teams of specialist hair cutters, extractors of gold from teeth, and burial/cremation units. Most work-Jews found that their reprieve from death seldom exceeded a few months. Poorly fed and frequently flogged, they suffered from dysentery and typhus. Anyone showing signs of sickness or weakness was likely to be sent to the gas chambers.

Stangl, first the Sobibor and then the Treblinka commandant, was a devoted family man and a devout Catholic, yet seems to have felt little sympathy for the victims. 'That was my profession', he said after the war. 'I enjoyed it. It fulfilled me.' Stangl's second in command at Treblinka, Kurt Franz, was described by (the very few) survivors as a sadist. A veteran of Buchenwald concentration camp and the T-4 programme, he trained his dog Barry to attack the genitals of his victims.

By the end of 1942 Himmler's goal of exterminating all the Polish Jews had been largely achieved. In December 1942 Belzec closed its gas chambers and the pace of killing at the other death camps slowed. The gas chambers at Auschwitz were now adequate to kill the rest of Europe's Jews. Globocnik's appointment to the post of SS leader in Istria in August 1943 marked the effective end of Operation Reinhard. By the end of November 1943, all the Operation Reinhard camps had been dismantled and the remaining work-Jews shot. Painstaking efforts were taken to obliterate every trace of the camps: the buildings were razed, the ground ploughed and pine trees planted. By the autumn of 1943, some 500,000 Jews are thought to have died at Belzec; 150,000-200,000 at Sobibor; and 900,000-1,200,000 at Treblinka. In November 1943 Himmler wrote to Globocnik as follows: 'I would like to express to you my thanks and appreciation for the great and unique service which you have performed for the whole German people by carrying out Operation Reinhard.'

9 Economic Considerations

The Operation Reinhard killings had a serious impact on Germany's war effort. The transportation of Jews to the death camps added extra pressure to Germany's railway system and hindered military transportation. More importantly, the killing affected Germany's potential labour pool. By 1942, the German empire was suffering from a desperate shortage of labour. German authorities in the General Government, as well as some Nazi ministers, realised that the killing of Jews was damaging Germany's industrial production, and argued in favour of retaining at least those Jews essential in terms of the war effort.

Some SS officials shared the economic concern. This was partly because the SS itself owned factories in the General Government and was a large employer of Jewish labour. By hiring out Jewish workers to firms on a daily basis, the SS also acquired a huge income. As a result of protests by the army, industry, civilian authorities and the SS, there were phases during which the extermination programme was slowed to permit the exploitation of Jewish labour, in line with the policy agreed at Wannsee. Hitler, however, usually discounted economic factors. In the autumn of 1942 he ordered the evacuation of even those Jews, in reserved occupations, who played a vital role in the war effort. Nevertheless, in 1941-2 two camps - Majdanek and Auschwitz - began to serve a dual purpose. On the one hand they were extermination centres: on the other they were labour camps in which Jews received a temporary stay of execution.

Primarily a labour camp for Poles and Russian prisoners, Majdanek (near Lublin) also contained at various times a large number of Jews. Some 60,000 of the 200,000 people who died at Majdanek were Jewish. In general, Jews were treated far worse than other prisoners. Inflicting cruelty on Jews was a semi-official policy of the camp and working the Jews to death seems to have been a more important aim than economic productivity. Jews were often ordered to perform useless tasks calculated to exhaust and shatter the health of even the strongest. The death rate for Jews was thus much higher than for non-Jews. In November 1943, the surviving Jews in Majdanek were shot as part of an operation code-named 'Harvest festival'.

10 Auschwitz

Auschwitz-Birkenau was originally created as a camp for Polish prisoners in 1940. By the end of 1941 it had expanded into an enormous labour camp, mainly for the utilisation of Soviet prisoners. In the late summer of 1941 Rudolf Hoess, the camp commandant, was told by Himmler that Auschwitz was to be a principal centre for killing Jews. Hoess had no moral qualms. A fanatical nationalist and member of the SS from 1934, he had worked his way up the career ladder in Dachau and Sachsenhausen concentration camps. Proud to have been singled out by Himmler, he was determined to carry out his orders to the best of his ability. Fretting about the practical mechanics of mass extermination, he hit upon the idea of using Zyklon B, consisting of small pellets of prussic acid crystals, as the gassing agent. First tested on Soviet prisoners, it proved deadly poisonous, killing in half the time required by carbon monoxide.

Given that the Auschwitz site was somewhat exposed, Hoess determined to shift the gassing to a new, more secluded camp, some three kilometres from the main site. This camp, known as Birkenau, was built around two old cottages. The windows of these were blocked up and airtight walls and doors added. Bunker 1 (the first cottage) began operations in early 1942. With good railway connections, Auschwitz-Birkenau was a convenient place to send Jews from most of Europe and quickly grew into the largest of the Nazi labour/extermination camps. It consisted ultimately of three main compounds: Auschwitz I, the original camp: Auschwitz II at Birkenau, the extermination camp; and Auschwitz III, the industrial centre at Monowitz. There were also dozens of satellite camps sprawling over a huge area.

The process of killing was slick and stream-lined. The transports arrived at a rail platform, located half way between Auschwitz I and

The main deportation railways to Auschwitz

Auschwitz II. (In April 1944 a direct rail spur was built to Birkenau.) An SS doctor, with a simple wave of the hand, decided who was fit and unfit. The fit were sentenced to hard labour in Auschwitz I or III. The unfit - the old, sick, children and mothers with young children - were condemned to immediate death in the gas chambers. The numbers of fit and unfit fluctuated, depending more on labour requirements than on physical health. But on average only about 30 per cent of each transport was seen as fit for work.

The victims were marched, or taken by truck, to Birkenau. The killing apparatus at Birkenau changed somewhat over time. The two gas chambers in Bunker 1 could accommodate 800 people at one go. Bunker 2, which contained three gas chambers holding 1,200 people, began operations in the summer of 1942. That summer Himmler also gave Hoess permission to build a new complex with four killing centres, containing a total of six gas chambers and 14 ovens, for cremating up to 8,000 corpses a day.

On reaching Birkenau, the victims were usually addressed in a friendly way and asked to undress quickly so they could take a bath. After undressing, they were herded into a gas chamber into which gas pellets were emptied through vents in the ceiling. The young and old usually died first as the gas saturated the lower part of the chamber. Stronger victims often struggled upward to better air, climbing over layers of bodies. But within 20 minutes all were dead. The SS doctor (who watched events through a peephole in the steel door) then gave the signal to switch on the ventilators that pumped the gas from the chamber and the *Sonderkommando* went in to clear the bodies.

Those prisoners pronounced fit for work were taken to Auschwitz I or III. While Jews formed a significant percentage of the population, the majority of the labour camps' inmates were non-Jews. By 1944 there were some 40 branch camps to which Jews might be sent. These camps supplied labour for some of the most famous German firms, including Krupp and Siemens-Schuckert. The largest industrial plant was a synthetic fuel and rubber complex, established by I.G.Farben, the petro-chemical combine, at Monowitz. Other work camps were run directly by profit-making SS agencies. For purposes of identification, prisoners (as in all other camps) were forced to display markings of different colours on their uniforms. This consisted of a number and a coloured triangle. A red triangle denoted a political prisoner, green a criminal, purple a Jehovah's Witness, black a 'shiftless element', pink a homosexual, and brown a Gypsy. Jews displayed a Star of David.

As in labour/concentration camps throughout German-occupied Europe, inmates of Auschwitz and its associated camps were stripped of their individuality and shorn of self-respect. Fed on watery soup and an ounce or two of bread, they endured primitive sanitary facilities and had practically no medicines, despite epidemics of typhus and other diseases. Prisoners were awakened at dawn and had to report for a roll call which might last for hours. They were then marched out to work. Most had to do hard manual labour at a murderous tempo and were subject to brutal punishment for the slightest breach of regulations or simply at the whim of the guards. Most of the managers of the German firms adopted SS methods and mentality. Given the conditions, few prisoners survived for more than a few months.

Some Auschwitz inmates were selected to serve as human guinea pigs for medical experiments. In 1942 Himmler, eager to find a method of mass sterilisation, sent Dr Carl Clauberg, a leading gynaecologist, to direct a research programme at Auschwitz. Clauberg's experiments involved injecting various chemicals into the ovaries of Jewish women. Other doctors subjected both men and women to massive doses of radiation which produced burns and effective sterilisation. Research papers, detailing the experiments which inflicted maiming or death on hundreds of prisoners, were then presented at medical meetings in Germany. The most infamous Auschwitz doctor was Josef Mengele - the 'Angel of Death'. Mengele was aged 32 when he arrived at the camp in 1943. He volunteered for duty at Auschwitz in order to pursue his research interest - the biology of racial differences. Selecting for study about 1,500 sets of identical twins, he used one of the twins for control while the other was used for experimentation purposes - as a laboratory researcher might use rats. Fewer than 200 twins survived his 'research'. (Similar experiments were conducted in other concentration camps. At Dachau, for example, prisoners were dumped into icy water, some naked and others dressed, to observe how their bodies would react and to see what might be done to revive them.)

11 The End of Auschwitz

By 1944 most Jews in German-occupied Europe had been killed. Only the Hungarian Jews had so far escaped the Holocaust. However, in the spring of 1944 Eichmann and his staff arrived in Budapest and mass deportations to Auschwitz began in May 1944. In less than a month some 289,000 Hungarian Jews were transported. Most (up to 12,000 a day) were killed immediately on arrival. In these circumstances, there were soon problems with the disposal of the corpses and the maintenance of secrecy. Hoess recalled:

1   In bad weather or a strong wind the smell of burning spread over
     several kilometres and caused the whole population of the surrounding
     area to start talking about the burning of Jews. ... Furthermore, the air
     defence authorities complained about the fire at night, which could
5   clearly be seen from the air. However, we had to keep cremating at night
     in order not to have to halt the incoming transports.[14]

In the summer and autumn of 1944, Himmler, working under the threat of imminent defeat, intensified German efforts to make Europe Jew-free. He combed some of the districts and camps previously overlooked, including Theresienstadt, the model concentration camp near Prague, which housed some 140,000 'privileged' Jews, among whom were prominent artists, intellectuals, and First World War veterans. By 1945 only 17,320 Jews remained at Theresienstadt: the rest had been sent to Auschwitz. Throughout October 1944 some 1,000 died each day in Auschwitz's gas chambers. Then on 2 November Himmler issued an order forbidding the further annihilation of Jews. Exactly why this order was issued remains uncertain. It may be that Germany was so short of labour that even Jewish workers were needed. Although the gassings stopped, the dying continued as the Germans squeezed the last ounce of productivity from the camp inmates. Meanwhile the Nazis tried to hide all traces of the killings, blowing up the gas chambers in the process.

On 17 January 1945 the last roll call at Auschwitz was held. The Germans counted 67,012 prisoners - less than half the total in August 1944. With the Russian army closing in, the Germans ordered the evacuation of all but about 6,000 inmates who were too young or infirm to move. The journey west for most of the 60,000 or so evacuees was dreadful. Those on foot received little food and were shot by the guards if unable to keep up. One march lasted 16 weeks and claimed the lives of all but 280 of the 3,000 who began it. Hundreds of those left behind in Auschwitz - without food or fuel - also died. When the Russians finally entered the camp on 27 January 1945 only 2,800 people remained alive. Many were so emaciated they died soon after liberation.

After the war, Hoess estimated the numbers of Jews killed at Auschwitz as follows: from Upper Silesia and the General Government - 250,000; from Germany - 100,000; from Holland - 95,000; from Belgium - 20,000; from France - 110,000; from Greece - 65,000; from Hungary - 400,000; and from Slovakia - 90,000.[15]

12 Other Deaths

The Jews were by no means the only group to suffer at the hands of the Germans. The Nazis planned to rid Germany and the occupied territories of all racial undesirables. In December 1942 Himmler signed an order by which all German Gypsies were to be deported to Auschwitz. Here they had their own special camp which soon had a population of over 10,000. The Gypsies initially fared better than the Jews. Few were immediately gassed and families were allowed to live together. However, in 1944 thousands of Gypsies were sent as labourers to other camps. In August 1944 the remaining 3,000 Gypsies at Auschwitz were gassed. Altogether some 200,000 Gypsies across Europe are thought to have been murdered during the war.

6,000 Jehovah's Witnesses, regarded as agents of a foreign power, were killed. So were large numbers of habitual criminals who were seen as being genetically preconditioned to a life of crime. (As many as 40,000 'criminals' may have been killed between 1939 and 1945.) The Nazis were also responsible for the deaths of colossal numbers of ordinary Poles and Russians. At least 10 million non-Jewish Russian civilians (and possibly as many as 25 million) died. Some of these deaths resulted from bombing and other military operations. But many died as a direct result of German occupation, reprisal and deportation policies. Of the 5.7 million Soviet prisoners captured in the war some 3.3 million died in German custody.

13 Forced Labour in Germany

By 1944 there were an astonishing eight million foreign workers in Germany - 25 per cent of the workforce. While some of these workers came voluntarily from countries which were Germany's allies, most came involuntarily from occupied countries. Foreign workers' treatment was largely determined by their racial origins. The 600,000 French workers, for example, were treated better than the 1.7 million Poles who, in turn, suffered less than the 2.8 million Russians. Many Poles and Russians worked in forced labour camps. Discipline in these camps was harsh, food and medical provision in short supply, and the tempo of work murderous.

Some Poles and Russians were hired out to private industry. Others were employed in agriculture and as domestic servants. (Half the Polish and Russian workers were women.) Working conditions depended on the type of job. Those employed in mining were far more likely to die than those working on farms. Some Germans treated their workers better than others. Most, it should be said, treated them savagely. Foreign workers stood a much greater chance of survival in country areas than in towns, where there was the constant threat of a bombing raid. Eastern workers were not allowed to enter public air raid shelters. Indeed, as far as possible the 'sub-human' Russians and Poles were isolated from Germans.

Such was the labour shortage by 1944 that Hitler even agreed to allow 100,000 Hungarian Jews to be brought to Germany to build huge underground bunkers in the Harz Mountains in which rockets and other important armaments were produced. The mortality rate among the Hungarian Jews was very high. The slogan of SS Dr Kammler was: 'Don't worry about the victims. The work must proceed ahead in the shortest time possible'.

14 The Situation in 1945

As the Soviet army advanced, the Germans were forced to abandon their labour camps in the east and move the inmates to camps further west. At least a third of the 700,000 inmates recorded in January 1945 probably lost their lives on these marches. About half the victims were Jews. The evacuees perished from cold, hunger, disease and periodic shootings. Some of the suffering may be explained by the chaos of the last days of the Third Reich. The destruction of road and rail links meant that it proved difficult to feed the prisoners. But the German guards, women as well as men, remained faithful to Nazi ideology, and, although not given orders to murder Jews, were quite happy to do so.

By 1944-5 Dachau and other German concentration camps, hitherto used primarily for non-Jewish prisoners and not equipped to kill large numbers of people, were used to house Jews evacuated from the east. While not systematically murdered, many Jews perished from starvation and disease. Conditions in the camps deteriorated considerably in the last weeks of the war as Germany collapsed. Allied soldiers who liberated the camps in west Germany (some of which contained few, if any, Jewish inmates) were appalled at what they found. American correspondent Edward Murrow delivered a famous radio broadcast describing conditions at Buchenwald in April 1945 on the day of its liberation.

1   There were 1,200 men in it [the barracks], five to a bunk. The stink was
    beyond all description. ...I asked how many men had died in the building
    during the last month. They called the doctor. We inspected his records.
    ... 242 out of 1,200, in one month ...
5   We went to the hospital. It was full. The doctor told me that 200 had
    died the day before. I asked the cause of death. He shrugged and said:
    'TB, starvation, fatigue, and there are many who have no desire to live.'
    ... [Another man] showed me the daily ration: one piece of brown
    bread about as thick as your thumb, on top of it a piece of margarine as
10 big as three sticks of chewing gum. That, and a little stew, was what they
    received every 24 hours.[16]

A British reporter, Patrick Gordon Walker, reported similarly on Belsen camp which was also liberated in April 1945:

1   Corpses in every state of decay were lying around, piled up on top of
    each other in heaps. ... People were falling dead all around, people who
    were walking skeletons. ... About 35,000 corpses were reckoned, more
    actually than the living. ... There was no food at all in the camp, a few
5   piles of roots - amidst the piles of dead bodies.[17]

15 Conclusion

The exact number of Jews who died in the Holocaust will never be known. There are no precise figures for those who were gassed, let alone for those who were massacred in the USSR or who died from malnutrition, disease or maltreatment. Gilbert's estimates (see page 4) are probably as good as any. Most of the killing was in 1942. In mid-

March 1942 some 75 per cent of all the eventual victims of the Holocaust were still alive: 25 per cent had already died. Less than a year later the situation was exactly reversed. Under 25 per cent still clung to a precarious existence. 'This is a page of glory in our history that has never been written and that is never to be written', Himmler told a group of SS officers in October 1943. In April 1945 Hitler declared that the killing of Europe's Jews was the most significant work he bequeathed to the German people. The fact that Hitler (who ordered the Holocaust) did not own up to it until the last days of the Third Reich, and Himmler (who ensured that Hitler's orders were carried out) said that details of it were 'never to be written', may simply be proof that both men were uncertain about the reaction of the German people. Or it may be that Hitler and Himmler, despite their intense anti-Semitic convictions, felt some unease about the morality of their actions. Whether their intense convictions lessen their guilt is a debate which is likely to continue as long as there are people on this planet.

References

1   R. Breitman, *The Architect of Genocide, Himmler and the Final Solution* (The Bodley Head, 1991), p. 153.
2   J. Noakes and G. Pridham (eds), *Nazism: 1919-1945: 3: Foreign Policy, War and Racial Extermination* (University of Exeter, 1988), p. 1090.
3   Christopher R. Browning, *The Final Solution and the German Foreign Office* (Holmes and Meier, 1978), p. 8.
4   Browning, *Path to Genocide*, p. 88.
5   Noakes and Pridham (eds), *Nazism*, vol. 3, p. 1104.
6   Burrin, *Hitler and the Jews: The Genesis of the Holocaust* (Arnold, 1994), p. 133.
7   Ian Kershaw, 'The Decision to Kill the Jews', in *History Review*, no. 12, p. 37.
8   Burrin, *Hitler and the Jews*, p. 144.
9   Noakes and Pridham (eds), *Nazism*, vol. 3, p. 1096.
10 Omer Bartov, 'Operation Barbarossa and the origins of the Final Solution', in David Cesarani (ed), *The Final Solution: Origins and Implementation* (Routledge, 1994), p. 123.
11 Noakes and Pridham (eds), *Nazism*, vol. 3, pp. 1100-1.
12 Ibid, p. 1093.
13 Ibid, p. 1135.
14 Ibid, p. 1183.
15 Ibid, p. 1189.
16 Louis L. Snyder, *Encyclopedia of the Third Reich* (McGraw-Hill, 1976), p. 44.
17 Ibid, p. 22.

Answering essay questions on 'The Final Solution: 1941-5'

Consider the following question:
> 'When did Hitler authorise the undertaking of the Final Solution?'

All essays should have a start, a middle and an end. Given that the middle paragraphs are the bulk of any essay it is obviously important that you get them right. Remember that each middle paragraph should focus on one relevant theme or issue. Remember also that in exam conditions most students struggle to produce more than seven or eight paragraphs. Bearing these thoughts in mind, which seven or eight themes/issues warrant a paragraph in the set question? Try composing first sentences for each of your paragraphs. It is, of course, implicit in this advice that the whole essay should answer the question set. You should not just narrate and describe in your middle paragraphs and then, in the final paragraph, answer the question. Hence you must have your overall interpretation worked out before you start the middle paragraphs, and these paragraphs should be written to support that interpretation. In this way you will avoid being irrelevant, and you will construct the sort of logical argument which gets good marks.

Source-based questions on 'The Final Solution: 1941-5'

1. Mass killing in the USSR

Read the extracts from von Reichenau, Hermann Graebe, and Rudolf Lange on pages 82-4 and examine the photographs on page 85. Answer the following questions:

a) Comment on Reichenau's view that the German soldier should be 'the supporter of a ruthless racial ideology and the avenger of all the bestialities which have been inflicted on the German nation and those ethnic groups related to it' (lines 6-9). (5 marks)

b) Does Reichenau's order prove that the army was fully implicated in the Holocaust? (4 marks)

c) To what extent is Hermann Graebe a reliable source? (6 marks)

d) Describe what seems to be happening in the photographic evidence. (5 marks)

e) To what extent do all the sources corroborate each other? (5 marks)

Summary Diagram
The Final Solution: 1941-5

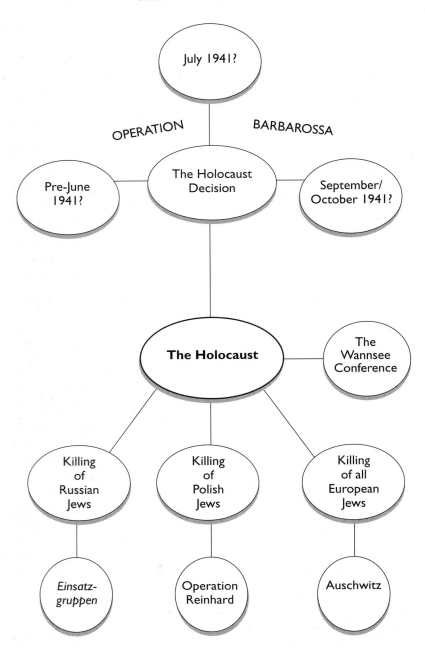

6 Who Else Was to Blame for the Holocaust?

1 Jewish Responsibility

By late-1942 many Jews were fully aware what 're-settlement in the east' meant. Yet most seem to have yielded to their fate with minimal resistance. Historian Raul Hilberg blamed the Jews - and particularly Jewish leaders - for not offering more in the way of resistance. In Hilberg's view the fact that Jews usually complied with Nazi decrees helped seal their fate. Hannah Arendt went further, arguing that Jewish leaders actually collaborated with the Germans in exterminating their own people. Without their assistance, she claimed, Nazi manpower would have been so overstretched that far fewer Jews would have died. 'The role of these leaders in the destruction of their own people', declared Arendt, ' is undoubtedly the darkest chapter of the whole dark story.'[1] Certainly much of the Holocaust process depended on Jewish participation. Jewish councils (or *Judensrate*) played a particularly important role in the German system - maintaining order, conveying German demands, making up deportation lists, and sometimes even informing the Nazis of the existence of resistance groups.

Jewish passivity undoubtedly made the job of the SS easier at every stage of the killing operations. However, most historians today are sympathetic to the plight of the Jews and far less critical of their leaders than Hilberg and Arendt. Until mid-1942 most Jews were not aware of what was happening in the east. It thus made sense to try to appease the Nazi authorities. When it was apparent that 'resettlement' was a euphemism for death, council leaders, in particular, faced a terrible dilemma. Knowing that armed resistance was tantamount to mass suicide, most saw no alternative but submission to the Germans. They clung to the hope that German policy might change and that at least part of their community might survive. The main charge against Jewish leaders is that they adopted the wrong tactics. In the circumstances, it is difficult to see what the right tactics were.

Most Polish and Russian Jews were killed before they had time to build effective resistance networks. Even those resistance groups which did materialise lacked arms and outside support. Polish Jews found it difficult to work with Polish partisans, who were often intensely anti-Semitic. The fact that Jews had trouble 'melting away' into a general population that feared German reprisals also limited resistance opportunities. Moreover, any resistance attempt simply resulted in massive German retaliation. Martin Gilbert cites the case of a young Jewish deportee in 1942 who attacked a Ukrainian guard with a dagger. The result of his action was that a trainload of deportees was immediately machine-gunned.[2]

Notwithstanding the problems, some historians now believe that there was more Jewish armed resistance, both by individuals and small groups, than was once thought to be the case. Some even claim that Jewish resistance was proportionately higher than that of most other Nazi victims, a remarkable fact considering the greater difficulties Jews encountered. (It is difficult to know the exact scale of Jewish involvement in resistance activity because Jews often fought in non-Jewish resistance groups.) While the results of the resistance activity were largely ineffective, few other people did much better. It is worth noting that 3,300,000 Soviet prisoners of war died while in German custody - shot, starved or worked to death. There was no serious uprising among these prisoners. If men of military age and training were unable to resist, Jewish communities of old men, women and children stood little chance.

The most serious Jewish resistance came in the Warsaw ghetto in April/May 1943. By 1943 most of Warsaw's Jews had been deported to Treblinka. The 60,000 or so survivors knew what to expect and some made preparations to fight. When German troops moved into the ghetto in mid-April 1943 in a 'final action' to make Warsaw Jew-free, they met armed resistance.With one rifle for every 150 men, the Jews had no illusions about the final outcome, but they chose to die fighting rather than die in the camps. Using the sewers and a network of specially built underground passages, a few Jews managed to hold out for nearly a month. The results were not successful. By May 1943 the Warsaw ghetto was virtually liquidated and over 56,000 Jews had been killed or transported to the camps. Only 16 Germans died in the fighting.

Successful armed resistance in the camps was virtually impossible. Most camp inmates were weakened by disease and starvation. The need to involve large numbers of inmates simply increased the risk of informers. Nevertheless, underground groups did meet to plan escape attempts. In August 1943 a few of Treblinka's work-Jews managed to break out. Most were quickly tracked down and executed. In October 1943 there was a mass escape from Sobibor in which at least 13 guards were killed. Although the Germans hunted down and shot most of the escapees, some 70 fugitives from Sobibor survived the war. That same month, a number of Jews in Auschwitz attacked and killed three guards. Some 450 Jewish prisoners died as a result of the incident.

The Germans deliberately used terror as a means to destroy the Jews mentally and physically. Psycho-historians once claimed that as a result many Jews 'regressed', developing types of behaviour which are the character of infancy, so much so that some came to accept the values of the SS as their own. Certainly many Jews became fatalistic, believing they could do little to influence their fate one way or another. But Jewish compliance was essentially governed by the hideous situation in which they found themselves. By no means all regressed. In the camps most prisoners concentrated their energies on the day-to-day struggle for food and on efforts to be allocated to an easy work detachment. The only chance of staying alive was to conform.

Although there was little armed resistance, Jews often did their best to subvert Nazi plans. Within the eastern ghettos, for example, German laws were subverted on a massive scale. There was considerable black market activity and clandestine meetings for a variety of reasons. Thousands of Jews escaped from ghettos into nearby forests. Facing German swoops, local peasant hostility, lack of provisions and harsh winters, survival for more than a few months in Poland was virtually impossible. In Russia Jews stood more chance of reaching Soviet partisan units. Of the 10,000 Jews who escaped from Minsk, about 5,000 survived the war.

After 1945 some European Jews bitterly criticised their brethren in Palestine and the USA for not doing more to help them. But many international Jewish communities did not at first believe the stories coming out of eastern Europe. The 500,000 Palestinian Jews, even when they realised the scale of the Holocaust, were divided on how to act. While some thought they should pull out every stop to help their brethren, others were more concerned with concentrating their efforts on creating a viable state in Palestine. It has been alleged that Palestinian Jews betrayed the Slovakian and Hungarian Jews by failing to provide the money crucial to the success of German schemes to ransom Jews. But it is far from certain that the Germans could be trusted or were even serious in offering negotiations. Nor, given American and British opposition, could any kind of deal have been easily struck. American Jewish leadership has been criticised for not pressurising the US government to do more to help the European Jews. But only 3.6 per cent of the American population was Jewish and American Jews had limited influence over President Roosevelt. It is thus hard to see what they could have done.

2 Non-German Responsibility

From 1940 to 1944 Germany dominated most of Europe. Even Germany's allies were very much under its thumb. The Germans pressed virtually all their allied and satellite states for Jewish deportees, claiming they were needed as forced labourers in the east. There were varying degrees of co-operation. After the war non-German collaborators at the highest level protested their innocence, claiming they were unaware of the ultimate intentions of the Germans or that they had little option but to obey German orders. Historians have tried to assess the extent to which various non-German governments - and people - knew about the real purpose of the deportations, and to what extent they collaborated.

a) Central and Eastern Europe

All the German satellites in central and eastern Europe - Slovakia, Croatia, Romania, Hungary and Bulgaria - had right-wing (but not necessarily strongly anti-Semitic) governments, each of which introduced measures against Jews in some form or another. These measures served two purposes: on the one hand they pleased Hitler; on the other, they also placated powerful, indigenous anti-Semitic groups, which modelled themselves on the Nazi Party. However, central and eastern European opinion was not uniformly hostile to Jews and each satellite state responded differently, sometimes with dramatically different results, to the varying degrees of German pressure.

The Slovakian government, led by Jozef Tiso (a Catholic priest), eager to demonstrate its co-operation in the building of a Nazi-dominated Europe, initially agreed to the deportation of the country's Jews. Tiso's government did become less co-operative on the Jewish front after 1942, but by then most Slovakian Jews were dead.

The pro-German leaders of Croatia happily introduced discriminatory legislation against Jews (considered pro-Serbian) in 1941. Thousands of Jews were shot or died in Croatian concentration camps from malnutrition, disease and terrible abuse. Some Jews were also sent to the Nazi death camps. Altogether about 30,000 Croatian Jews are thought to have died. The Croatians were also concerned with 'ethnically cleansing' their new country of Serbs and Bosnians. During the war over 400,000 Serbs were deliberately killed by the Croats using measures similar to the *Einsatzgruppen* in the USSR.

In 1941-2 Romanian dictator Ion Antonescu created an atmosphere where the killing of Jews was encouraged even if not specifically ordered. Over 100,000 Jews were killed by Rumanian forces in the provinces of Bukovina and Bessarabia (recovered from the USSR). Many died on terrible marches to camps and ghettos in a region known as Transnistria. No other country beside Germany was involved in the massacre of Jews on such a scale. However, as the defeat of Germany became a distinct possibility, Antonescu rejected German pressure to deport native Romanian Jews to the Nazi death camps. This allowed him to claim after the war that he had saved most of the 300,000 Romanian-born Jews, a claim which obscured the other half of the story.

Bulgaria, which had no strong anti-Semitic tradition, refused to hand over Jews who were Bulgarian citizens. Interestingly more Jews were alive in Bulgaria at the end of the war than at the start.

Until 1944 the Hungarian government, headed by Admiral Horthy, was deaf to Germany's deportation requests. Hungary thus seemed something of a safe haven for Jews fleeing from Germany, Austria, Poland and Czechoslovakia. (Hungary's Jewish population increased from 400,000 in 1939 to near 700,000 in 1944.) However, many

Hungarians were anti-Semitic. Some Jews suffered terribly in Hungarian labour battalions before 1944 and Hungarian troops willingly participated in the massacre of Soviet Jews. In March 1944 German forces occupied Hungary and Eichmann immediately implemented a swift deportation programme, as a result of which 430,000 Jews were sent to Auschwitz. In July Horthy, concerned about western reaction, suspended deportations. However, he was overthrown by the Germans in October and the new pro-Nazi government continued the slaughter of Jews until the USSR overran most of Hungary in early 1945.

b) Western Europe

The situation was similarly patchy in western Europe. Once the deportations began in the summer of 1942, the Germans relied heavily on native police and bureaucrats. Remarkably few Germans were available for such work: fewer than 3,000 German civilians, for example, managed occupied France in August 1941. By 1942 local officials had acquired the habit of working with the German authorities with the result that many hardly thought twice about maintaining the pattern of collaboration when it came to rounding up Jews to be sent eastwards. However, the degree of co-operation was to vary considerably and this, in part, determined the widely different Jewish losses - from 75 per cent of Jews in Holland to only 5 per cent in Denmark.

France had a strong anti-Semitic tradition and the right-wing Vichy government, led by Pétain, quickly introduced measures to eliminate Jewish economic and political influence. These measures were taken voluntarily: they were not in response to German orders. By 1942 the Vichy government had effectively outlawed Jews, taking most of their property and interning many in special camps in the process. For those French officials who collaborated with the Germans in 1942, the deportations were simply a continuation of a programme deemed by the Vichy government to be in France's national interest. About half of France's 300,000 Jews did not have French citizenship and many Frenchmen were happy to lend a hand to rid their country of unwanted outsiders. However, while the Vichy government was willing to deport foreign Jews, it resisted Germany's attempts to deport French-born Jews. Thus the number of Jews deported from France was restricted to under 80,000.

Unlike the Vichy government, Danish political leaders were adamantly opposed to all aspects of Nazi anti-Semitism. Until 1943, the Germans did not interfere much in internal Danish affairs and so Jews remained relatively safe. But in August 1943, following a general crisis in Danish-German relations, German authorities insisted on Jewish persecution. However, most of Denmark's 8,000 Jews, helped by thousands of Danes, managed to escape to Sweden in an armada of small boats in the autumn of 1943.

By 1943, when there was an increasing awareness of what deportation actually meant, officials across western Europe proved less reliable and the Germans could not sustain the 1942 momentum. Nevertheless, some 40 per cent of west European Jews were killed. (Holland, with 105,000 Jews deported, suffered the greatest loss both in absolute and relative terms.) The extent to which west European collaborationists were in a position to say 'no' to the Nazis remains debatable. The claim that the situation would have been much worse without the collaborationists has a certain plausibility. In France, for example, far more Jews survived the Holocaust than died. This was in part due to delaying tactics adopted by the Vichy government. Had Pétain's government done more to resist German pressure, the Nazis might have replaced it with a government which would have proceeded far more energetically against the Jews.

c) Italy

The Nazis encountered serious obstacles in Italy where anti-Semitism had never been strong and where most of the 50,000 Jews were fully integrated into Italian society. Indeed Mussolini's Fascist Party had considerable Jewish support in the 1920s and early 1930s. Mussolini, while not particularly liking Jews, shared the indifference of most Italians to a 'problem' which he did not think existed. In 1938 he did issue a number of anti-Jewish laws but persecution was mild and it was clear that the measures were not particularly popular. During 1941-2 the Italian-occupied part of France became a haven for some 50,000 Jews, protected by Italian police against both German and French police. This protection did not survive the German take-over of northern Italy, following Italy's surrender to the Allies in September 1943. Jews from the French-Italian zone and elsewhere were rounded up and sent to Auschwitz. This measure was entirely a German operation. Even Italian Fascist authorities did not readily co-operate.

d) Poland and the USSR

There were no collaborationist governments in Nazi-occupied Poland and the USSR to facilitate the Holocaust. Here German authorities determined their own priorities. However, the attitude of local people to Jews had some bearing on the Holocaust. The subject of Polish-Jewish relations in wartime Poland is a controversial area. Polish writers tend to minimise Polish anti-Semitism. Jewish historians, by contrast, label most Poles as anti-Semitic and claim they did little to help, and much to harm, the Jews during the war. Poland certainly had a long anti-Semitic tradition and most Poles do seem to have been indifferent to Jewish suffering. Some actually approved of the Holocaust. It was not unusual for Poles to attack and kill Jewish fugitives, and, rather than sheltering Jews, Poles were far more likely to inform the Germans of their whereabouts. However, the reality of Nazi terror was so overwhelming that opportunities to assist Jews were more limited in Poland than anywhere else in occupied Europe. Those Poles caught helping Jews faced certain death.

Many people in the Ukraine and the Baltic States were vehemently anti-Semitic. Regarding the Jews as Soviet agents, some of the national groups in the former USSR were ready to collaborate with the Germans, whom they initially saw as liberators. In Lithuania, in particular, there were spontaneous local attacks on Jews - many of whom had supported the unpopular Soviet regime in Lithuania in 1940-1. Over 90 per cent of all Lithuanian Jews were killed: possibly as many as two-thirds were killed by Lithuanians. Throughout much of German-occupied Soviet territory local paramilitary forces willingly took part in massacring Jews.

e) Conclusion

There is no doubt that the strength of European anti-Semitism eased the Nazi implementation of the Holocaust. The intensity of anti-Semitism in any particular country also had some effect on how far the destruction process went. In the final analysis, however, the degree of Nazi control, rather than the strength of local anti-Semitism, was the decisive factor in determining the number of Jews who were killed. Holland, for example, which was far less anti-Semitic than Romania, had a much higher rate of Jewish losses. In Poland, where the Nazis brutally enforced their rule, millions of Jews were murdered. In Finland, where the Nazis had no real power, none of the country's 2,000 Jews were killed. (Finland was the only country among Germany's allies and satellites which succeeded in protecting its Jews completely.)

3 Allied Responsibility

Despite German efforts to maintain secrecy, word about the Holocaust quickly leaked to the outside world. As early as June 1942 the *Daily Telegraph* in Britain reported that the Germans had gassed 700,000 Jews. News of German atrocities continued to be fully reported in Britain and the USA throughout late 1942 and until the end of the war. This prompts several questions. Why was so little done to help the Jews? Were Allied leaders indifferent to the fate of the Jews, simply lacking in imagination about how to help them, or essentially helpless?

Historians Arthur Morse and David Wyman have launched scathing attacks on Allied (but especially American) leaders for 'abandoning' the Jews. They assert that both Britain (which had problems in Palestine) and the USA (where anti-Semitism was strong) feared a flood of Jewish immigrants. Thus the US State Department and the

British Foreign Office - both of which contained personnel who held disparaging attitudes towards Jews - are accused of making only limited efforts to assist the Jews. In Morse and Wyman's view, more could have been done to pressure Germany and its satellite states to release the Jews. Stern threats of post-war retribution might have helped (in fact, possibly did help) the situation in Romania and Hungary. More might have been done to encourage neutral countries (like Spain and Switzerland) to take extra Jews. More publicity about the Holocaust could have been disseminated through Europe, urging Jews to hide, fight or flee. Ransom overtures might have been more thoroughly investigated. Wyman is particularly critical of President Roosevelt, claiming that his indifference to the Holocaust was the worst failure of his presidency. Not until 1944 did Roosevelt establish a War Refugee Board, the specific task of which was to help save Jews. Although this Board later claimed it had saved some 200,000 Jewish lives, in reality it received little in the way of funding. Roosevelt rarely commented on the Holocaust. His indifference seems to have reflected the wider indifference of the American public. Opinion polls conducted during the war suggest that nearly half of Americans believed that Jews had too much power and influence within the USA. Allied military leaders have also been charged with rejecting several appeals to bomb Auschwitz and the railroads to it, the assumption being that such an act would have saved many Jewish lives.

However, Morse and Wyman's criticisms are probably unfair. The notion that the western world erected an almost insuperable barrier to Jewish emigrants is simply wrong. The reality was that some 70 per cent of German, Austrian and Czech Jews had managed to flee from the Third Reich before September 1939. 160,000 Jews found refuge in Britain and its empire/commonwealth, especially in 1938-9, in what Rubinstein has described as 'one of the greatest rescues of any beleaguered group in history'.[3] Only about 130,000 Jews remained in the 1933 borders of Germany in 1941 when Hitler - not Churchill or Roosevelt - stopped Jewish emigration.

In fairness to Roosevelt, he did not appreciate the full extent of Nazi policies until late in the war. Like most contemporaries (including US Jewish leaders), he thought that the genocide stories were anti-German propaganda and was unable to grasp that something remarkably different from previous massacres was occurring in Nazi-controlled Europe. Most American newspaper editors were similarly sceptical. Aware of exaggerated British propaganda stories in the First World War, they were reluctant to accept as gospel truth second- and third-hand reports, especially when they came via the USSR. Ordinary Americans (and Britons) found events in a remote part of Poland easy to disbelieve and dismiss from their consciousness.

Once there was government acceptance of the atrocities, there was still a major problem of what to do. The war conditions made rescue of the seven million Jews in Poland and the USSR impossible. The ransom of Jews was really a non-starter. While it is possible that the Germans might have been willing to negotiate for Jewish lives in Hungary in 1944, Allied leaders were - rightly - suspicious of the proposals. They had no intention of being blackmailed by the Nazis or giving Hitler war materials in exchange for Jews. This might simply have led to a lengthening of the war and more casualties. Moreover any negotiations with Hitler simply increased Stalin's suspicions and risked disrupting the anti-German alliance. The Allies lacked the military capacity to have bombed Auschwitz before 1944 - never mind the fact that the camp had remained a well-kept secret until then! The bombing of Auschwitz in 1944, even if successful, would have come too late to have saved most of the camp's victims. Even if Auschwitz had been successfully bombed (or its rail traffic successfully disrupted), it is likely that the Germans would have found other means of killing. Moreover, given that aerial bombing was rarely pin-point accurate, bombing Auschwitz might have resulted in thousands of deaths. (In 1944 most Jewish organisations strongly opposed the bombing of Auschwitz on the grounds it would kill more Jews than it saved.) Targeting Auschwitz would also have diverted Allied air forces from their real mission of destroying the strategic industries that sustained the Nazi war machine. Allied leaders were convinced that the best way to help the Jews was to win the war as quickly as possible. This made sense. If the war had ended a year earlier, the Hungarian Jews might well have survived. If it had continued another year, more Jews would certainly have died.

Britain has been particularly condemned for its unwillingness to allow more Jews to settle in Palestine. However, before 1936 Britain allowed Jewish emigrants almost free access to Palestine. After 1936, aware that any great influx of Jews into Palestine would alienate both the native Palestinians and neighbouring Arab states, the British government was more circumspect. In May 1939 it limited Jewish emigrants to 75,000 over the next five years. However, it is unlikely that British concerns over Palestinian immigration impeded efforts to rescue Jews: the key fact is that after 1939 there were precious few Jews who had the opportunity of escaping to Palestine. The British government broadcast the news of the killings all over the world and also issued solemn warnings that the war crimes' perpetrators would be severely punished. It is hard to see what more it could have done.

4 Papal Responsibility

Serious charges have been levied against Pope Pius XII for not speaking out in defence of the Jews and for not explicitly condemning either the Holocaust or the massacres of Serbs in Croatia. The Vatican, with its excellent contacts with Poland and its unrivalled net of informants all over Europe, was well aware of what was going on. Although Pius's policy of neutrality was in line with the longstanding tradition of Vatican diplomacy, it is difficult to defend his silence. Many Germans, Austrians and Croats were sincere Catholics and a papal appeal not to co-operate with the Nazis might have had some effect. Instead, Pius XII (who feared the threat of communism more than the threat of fascism) expressed no views on the great moral issue, not just of the day but perhaps of the century. This silence surely did amount to complicity. Moreover, in Slovakia and Croatia, both avowedly Catholic states, Catholic bishops gave massive support to governments which were fully supporting genocide. Only when it was clear that the Nazis were definitely losing the war did the Pope finally speak out and sympathise with the plight of the Jews. It should be said that Protestant Church leaders in Germany had no better record: indeed many supported the Nazi regime.

5 Neutral Responsibility

Throughout the war neutral governments were in a unique position to aid the Jews either by receiving refugees or trying to implement diplomacy which might have saved thousands of Jews. Broadly speaking the actions of Spain, Sweden, Switzerland and Turkey show few instances of real concern for the Jews. Vulnerable militarily and economically, most neutral states feared offending Hitler. Not until 1944, when German defeat seemed increasingly likely, did the policy of neutrals begin to shift. Sweden, Spain and even Switzerland began to take in more Jewish refugees. But before then the Swiss, in particular, had turned away thousands of Jews - to near certain death. In the summer and autumn of 1944 diplomats from Spain, Sweden, Turkey and Switzerland did participate in an unusual - and successful - rescue mission in Hungary. In an attempt to protect the 200,000 Jews still remaining in Budapest, they issued thousands of letters of protection intended to safeguard the bearers. They then secured the recipients in hundreds of special apartment buildings. In this way some 100,000 Jews were saved. A key figure was Raoul Wallenberg, attache of the Swedish legation in Budapest. Arriving in July 1944, he personally issued safe-conduct passes to hundreds of Jews and also proved adept at cajoling or bribing officials to ensure that Hungarian authorities respected the safe havens. Ironically Wallenberg was arrested by the Russians when they 'liberated' Budapest in January 1945 and, suspected of espionage, died in a Soviet prison in the late 1940s.

References
1   H. Arendt, *Eichmann in Jerusalem: A Report on the Banality of Evil* (Viking, 1963), p.117-118.
2   M. Gilbert, *Atlas of the Holocaust* (Michael Joseph, 1982), p. 115.
3   W. Rubinstein, the *Daily Mail,* Saturday, 5 July 1997, p.16.

Summary Diagram
Who Else Was to Blame for the Holocaust?

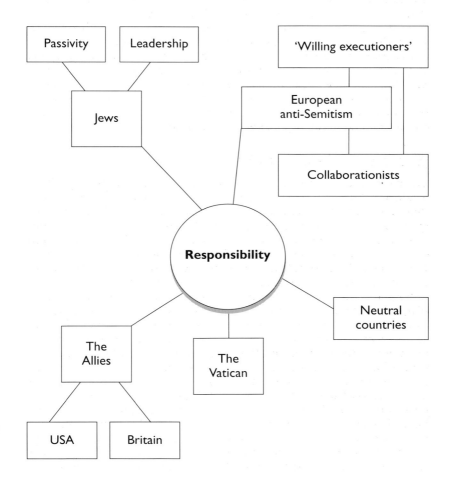

7 Conclusion: German Responsibility

1 Hitler's Responsibility

Most Holocaust historians today position themselves at some point between the extreme 'intentionalist' and 'functionalist' poles. Few now think that Hitler envisaged and planned the Final Solution from 1933 onwards. Only in retrospect have the anti-Semitic measures pre-1941 acquired the appearance of being part of a systematic escalation of persecution which was intended to end in extermination. Nevertheless, most historians agree that Hitler's fervent anti-Semitism played a central role in the evolution of Nazi Jewish policy. There is no doubt that he approved the cumulative intensification of Jewish persecution and that his attitude served as its legitimating authority. While not always personally concerned with the detailed moves to achieve a 'solution of the Jewish Question', he gave signals that established priorities and goals.

Hitler's actions down to 1941 do not indicate that he was set on murdering all of Europe's Jews. Until 1941 all the leading Nazi officials concerned with the Jewish issue - Himmler, Heydrich, Frank and Goering - declared that a policy of compulsory emigration offered the only real solution to the Jewish question and they acted accordingly. The idea of Jewish reservations, whether in Madagascar or in the 'east' were taken seriously. There is no basis for the claim that such plans were simply designed to conceal the regime's genocidal intention.

Nevertheless, given Hitler's hatred of Jews, the potential for a 'war of racial destruction' was always there. Operation Barbarossa provided Hitler with both the opportunity and justification to solve the Jewish problem once and for all. Given the apocalyptic nature of the struggle, it made sense (by Hitler's standards) to exterminate Russian Jews and then to go a stage further and order the killing of all European Jews. The debate about whether the Holocaust decision (or decisions) resulted from the euphoria of success or rather from fear born of defeat looks set to continue. As Kershaw has said: 'Given the nature of and gaps in the evidence, and the secrecy and camouflage language used by Nazi leaders even amongst themselves, it is likely that an answer to these fundamental questions will always rest on the balance of probabilities.'[1]

Presumably because he feared alienating the German public, Hitler tried to conceal his own personal responsibility for the slaughter. (He did much the same with the euthanasia killings.) Both in public and in private, he continued to insist that the Jews were being 'resettled' or being mobilised for 'appropriate labour duties'. No order signed by Hitler containing an explicit command to exterminate the Jews has so far come to light. It is unlikely to do so. Almost certainly there never was a written order. This was not the way that Hitler operated. Incredible though it may seem, the order to kill millions of people may have been little more than a nod from Hitler to Himmler. But the Holocaust decision was undoubtedly Hitler's. The Final Solution would have been unthinkable without his express authorisation.

2 Himmler, Heydrich and the SS

While Hitler was the ideological and political author of the Holocaust, it was translated from a dream into a concrete programme by Himmler, Heydrich and the SS. Most of the SS - 800,000 strong in 1944 - were not directly involved in the mass killing. Nor was the SS the only organisation responsible for the Holocaust: other power centres, like the *Wehrmacht* and the administrations in the occupied territories, participated in the killings. Nevertheless, the SS played a crucial role. Himmler was able to commit SS resources and manpower to planning, constructing and operating the death camps, and SS units were also responsible for much of the killing in the USSR. Few SS men agonised over the slaughter. Most believed they were doing their duty. This enabled them to retain a sense of moral integrity. (Few were sadists or psychopaths.) Himmler's conviction of the righteousness of the cause is revealed in the following extract from a speech to SS leaders in October 1943:

1   I also want to talk to you quite frankly about a very grave matter. We can talk about it quite frankly among ourselves and yet we will never speak of it publicly. ... I am referring to the Jewish evacuation programme, the extermination of the Jewish people. It is one of those
5   things which are easy to talk about. 'The Jewish people will be exterminated', says every party comrade. ... And then they come along, the worthy 80 million Germans and each of them produces his decent Jew. ... Not one of those who talk like that has watched it happening, not one of them has been through it. Most of you will know what it means when
10   100 corpses are lying side by side, or 500 or 1,000 are lying there. To have stuck it out and - apart from a few exceptions due to human weakness - to have remained decent, that is what has made us tough.[2]

Himmler and Heydrich were not the only Nazi leaders who played a major role in the Holocaust. Other leading Nazis vigorously supported harsh anti-Semitic measures. Some, like Goering, may have done so more to enhance their own prestige and extend their own authority than for any great conviction. But others, like Goebbels, were vehemently anti-Semitic. The extent to which all the leading Nazis were implicated in the Holocaust remains a subject of debate. At the Nuremberg trials, only a few of the 21 main defendants acknowledged their culpability. Some, like Albert Speer, claimed ignorance of the Holocaust. But most leading Nazis were almost certainly aware of what was going on in the east. Whether men like Speer, who may have recognised that the Holocaust was an evil, were more or less guilty than men like Himmler, who believed it was a positive good, is a moot point.

3 The Euthanasia Connection

The euthanasia - or T-4 - killings were an important precedent for the Holocaust. Many of the T-4 personnel were very much involved in the Final Solution - from Philipp Bouhler and Viktor Brack downwards. At least 90 men who learned their trade in the euthanasia centres of Brandenburg, Grafenek and Hartheim staffed the death camps of Belzec, Sobibor and Treblinka. The killing technique developed by T-4 was replicated in the Final Solution. The T-4 programme also showed that individuals, largely selected at random, would carry out mass killings without scruple.

4 The German Army and Police

Historians now agree that regular army units provided essential support for the *Einsatzgruppen* in the USSR in 1941-2. The army high command accepted the need for harsh measures against both Jews and communists - seen as the same deadly enemy. Army and SS leaders worked collaboratively in the occupied Russian territory. Pity and softness were seen as dangerous weaknesses: all measures were justified in the battle against Jewish-Bolshevism. Army actions thus took on the aspect more of an extension of Nazi racial policies than of operations according to military procedures. One example suffices. The 707th Infantry Division in one month shot 10,431 Russian 'captives' out of a total of 10,940. While it claimed partisan activity as the excuse, the division suffered only seven casualties - two dead and five wounded - in the same period.[3]

The 15,000 men in the police battalions also played a crucial role in the mass shootings. Both Christopher Browning and Daniel Goldhagen have focused attention on the members of Reserve Police Battalion 101. (Thanks to war crimes investigations, plenty of evidence - largely testimonies from surviving members - was collected in the 1960s and 1970s.) The killers of Reserve Police Battalion 101 were a near-perfect cross section of Third Reich society - skilled and unskilled workers, shop-keepers, farmers, and a few civil servants, middle managers and academics. Browning and Goldhagen both stress the 'ordinariness' of the Germans in the unit. They were certainly not an elite who had been selected for the killing because of military or ideological fitness. Most were not fanatical Nazis. Barely one in 30 was a member of the SS. Only a third were members of the Nazi Party (much the same as the national average). Some had probably voted socialist or communist before 1933. The average age of Police Battalion 101 was 36: most of the men had families and children; many were unfit or too old for proper military service.

The men of Police Battalion 101 were not trained especially for the killing. Their ideological training amounted to two hours a week. Even the officers were not hard-core Nazis. Thus the Police Battalion was not a promising group from which to recruit mass murderers. Yet this is what most of the men willingly became - killing not in a depersonalised way but at very close quarters, so that they were often splattered with the blood of their victims - babies, children and women. Most killed without pity, often humiliating and torturing their victims first. Their own testimony reveals that they revelled in their victims' slaughter - crowding them into barns and then setting fire to them; making them dance and crawl before shooting them; and burying them alive. None of the men were forced to act in this way. Cruelty was not an order of the state. Those who were squeamish could ask to be transferred to other duties. Refusal to take part in the killing did not necessarily result in punishment or even damage career prospects. Peer group pressure - a pride in toughness and manliness - coupled with a general approval of genocide seems to have motivated most of the men, who actually took pride in their accomplishments and did not hide what they were doing from their loved ones at home. Goldhagen's conclusion is that because the men of Police Battalion 101 were so representative of German society, the 'inescapable truth' is that most of their fellow Germans would also have served as Hitler's 'willing executioners'.[4]

The mentality of those involved in the killing is shown in the following letter, written in June 1942 (in the Ukraine) and sent by a young, happily married, police sergeant (who missed his wife and family) to an SS chief, a friend from his home district:

1 We men of Germany must be strict with ourselves even if it means a long period of separation from our family. For we must finish matters once and for all and finally settle accounts with the war criminals, in order to create a better and eternal Germany for our heirs. ...There are
5 three or four operations a week. Sometimes Gypsies, another time Jews, partisans and all sorts of trash. ...

I am grateful for having been allowed to see this bastard race close up. If fate permits, I shall have something to tell my children. Syphilitics, cripples, idiots were typical of them. One thing was clear: they were
10 materialists to the end. They were saying things like: 'We are skilled workers, you are not going to shoot us.' They were not men but monkeys in human form. ...We are ruthlessly making a clean sweep with a clear conscience.[5]

5 The Bureaucracy

Historian Raul Hilberg claimed that the Final Solution was essentially an administrative process involving the participation of bureaucrats from every sphere of organisation in Germany. The bureaucrats were thus an essential part of what Hilberg termed the 'machinery of destruction' which, once set in motion, just ground on ineluctably, generating its own momentum and needing no operator. After the war, most bureaucrats - diplomats, civil servants, railway officials - claimed that they were not aware of - or responsible for - the end result of their labours. (Adolf Eichmann, the deportation supremo, on trial for his life in Jerusalem, said that his authority extended only as far as the gates of Auschwitz: not beyond.) Certainly the path to complicity in mass murder was not marked by a single dramatic turning point: it was gradual - an almost imperceptible descent past the point of no return. The official language of the regime also helped camouflage what was happening. Nevertheless, many officials probably did know what fate awaited the Jews in the east. Few seem to have agonised over their work: most seem to have been committed to the task in hand.

6 To What Extent Were Ordinary Germans to Blame?

After 1945 it was very convenient for Germans to blame Hitler for everything that had happened in the Third Reich. Those Germans who were directly involved in the killing claimed that they were mere cogs in the machine and had no choice but to obey orders. Most Germans said they had no idea what was happening in the east. Historians tended to accept this disclaimer. The general assumption was that, while many Germans were anti-Semitic, most would have drawn the line at genocide had they known of it. Historians today, however, are less sure. Some think that many Germans were not only aware of but actually supported the mass killings. To what extent should the German people as a whole be held collectively responsible for the Holocaust?

a) The Case for the Germans

Many historians believe that Germans voted for Hitler in the early 1930s not because they were anti-Semitic but for other reasons - not least economic considerations. There is also evidence that the Nazis sometimes found it hard to mobilise anti-Semitism after 1933. The spring 1933 boycott was a failure in this respect. After 1941 most Germans probably did believe the official government line that the Jews were simply being resettled in labour camps: compulsory labour service was part of everyday life in Nazi Germany. The Holocaust occurred out of sight of most Germans. Most were reluctant to believe the rumours. (News of the Holocaust was accepted with similar scepticism by western public opinion.) The killing was done by a small number of zealous activists. Given the nature of the Nazi regime, there was little that ordinary Germans could do to oppose anti-Semitic policies. Even so a few Germans did risk their lives helping Jews to escape 're-settlement'.

It can also be said in mitigation that the war produced a blunting of moral feeling among Germans, as it did with Britons and Americans, few of whom felt any qualms about bombing German cities or even atom-bombing Hiroshima and Nagasaki. Historian Ernst Nolte has argued that the Holocaust should be viewed in the context of the time. It was not a unique act. After 1917 Soviet governments tried to exterminate a whole class of people. Nolte has suggested that the Holocaust should be seen, in part at least, as a response to Bolshevik mass murder. Germans acted out of self-defence against an enemy who was also waging a war of annihilation. Perhaps the best defence of the German people is the fact that Hitler tried to preserve the secrecy of the Holocaust because he was not sure that he could rely on popular support.

b) The Case Against the Germans

Many of the basic ideas of Nazism had wide popularity in Germany before Hitler came to power. That was why he achieved power. Large numbers of Germans were anti-Semitic before 1933 - most moderately, some vehemently. Many Nazi activists joined the Party simply because of its anti-Semitism. Many of Germany's most important elites - the civil service, the army, the churches - were strongly anti-Semitic. Even among the Nazis' opponents there was considerable anti-Semitism. Nazi propaganda after 1933 probably increased this pervading anti-Semitism. After 1933 the Nazi regime seems to have had a large measure of support from broad sections of the population. Hitler's popularity, while partly the result of propaganda, was largely the result of his perceived success and the fact that Nazism embodied many of the basic attitudes of the German people. 'In short, the regime confirmed and enforced the values and prejudices of a substantial section of the population.'[6] Ian Kershaw's work has shown that, in some respects, the Nazis failed to dragoon public opinion into complete conformity. Some Germans did express criticism of some aspects of Hitler's rule. (There was opposition to euthanasia, for example.) But very few Germans, not even Protestant or Catholic clergy, were critical of anti-Semitic action at any stage between 1933 and 1945.

Knowledge about the mass shootings in the USSR was fairly widespread. German soldiers and police who had actually witnessed or participated in the killings told their families when they returned home on leave. The Allied governments also did their best to inform Germans of the Holocaust by radio broadcasts and leaflet drops. A general awareness that dreadful things were happening to Jews was sufficient to make people worried about retaliatory measures that might be taken against Germany if it lost the war. At best the fate of the Jews seems to have been of only minimal interest to most Germans: this indifference might, in itself, be seen as passive complicity in terms of what happened to the Jews. At worst, it could be that many Germans actually approved of the Holocaust. The killing could not have happened without the co-operation of many 'ordinary' German men and women. (Many of the guards in the 1944-5 death marches were women who proved to be just as brutal as their male counterparts.) Most Germans identified with Hitler's goals. After 1941 most Germans saw Jews and communists as one and the same enemy against whom they were fighting a war to the death. In the eyes of many Germans, the only good Jew was a dead one. Those Germans who did help the Jews were a very small minority.

Given the nature of Nazi rule, it is remarkably difficult to measure mass opinion in Germany after 1933. However, it does seem fair to say that deep-rooted German anti-Semitic beliefs were a (if not *the*) 'central causal agent of the Holocaust'.[7] Clearly not all members of the German nation should be held to bear an equal share of responsibility. Some probably did not know - or approve of - what was going on. Nevertheless, most were well aware that terrible measures were being taken against the Jews. At worst, most approved of those measures. At best, most were indifferent.

7 Conclusion

Although the Holocaust was an enterprise to which countless people throughout Europe contributed, it was essentially a German enterprise. The German people as a whole, therefore, (pre-1945) share a major collective responsibility for what happened to European Jewry. The easy way to escape responsibility after 1945 was to lay all the blame at the door of Adolf Hitler. Hitler was a very convenient scapegoat - simply because he was also the main guilty individual. Animated by intense convictions, he played a pivotal role in bringing about the Holocaust. His personality, leadership style and ideological convictions shaped the nature of the Third Reich. His racist dogma was the critical engine of the Nazi state. Anti-Semitism in Germany as a whole may have been a necessary condition for the Holocaust but it was not a sufficient one. In the end it was Hitler that made the difference. As Marrus says: 'No Hitler: No Holocaust.'[8]

Hitler was not totally driven by ideology: he could and did act opportunistically. However, long-term goals and an opportunistic approach are not incompatible. While Hitler probably did not always harbour the intention of literally exterminating the Jews, extermination was always a possibility, especially in the event of war. And Hitler wanted war. It was the 'father of all things' - 'the unalterable law of the whole of life - the prerequisite for the natural selection of the strong and the precedent for the elimination of the weak.'[9] He probably did not want the war he got in 1939. But he certainly got the war he wanted in 1941. Operation Barbarossa was the key to the Holocaust. The war against the USSR gave him the opportunity of winning *lebensraum* and at the same time of destroying Judeo-Bolshevism. From June 1941 onwards his ideologically motivated anti-Semitism could be declared a military necessity.

While European anti-Semitism in general and German anti-Semitism in particular might have been essential pre-conditions, it is difficult to see how anti-Semitism by itself could have led to the Holocaust. The remorseless logic of Hitler's ideology led ultimately to the Final Solution. Given Hitler's hatred of the Jews, and the fact that he blamed them for Germany's defeat in the First World War, it is hard to imagine him settling for any other solution once Germany attacked the USSR - something he always hoped to do. The road to Auschwitz was not necessarily very twisted. Its completion had to wait until the conditions were right. The moment they were, Hitler commissioned his architect-builders - Himmler and Heydrich - to design and construct the road.

Burrin poses the question: 'If Hitler had died in the summer of 1941, would the final solution have taken place?'. He concludes that 'Without him, the decisive thrust would probably have been absent.'[10] Hitler was thus largely responsible for what happened. Indeed, he would wish to be remembered for that responsibility. What to most people now seems totally irrational and evil seemed to Hitler logical and good. Traditional ethics and morality were turned inside out. At the very end of his life he claimed with pride that the extermination of the Jews was his legacy to the world.

References

1   I. Kershaw, 'The Decision to Kill the Jews', *History Review*, no. 12, 1992, p. 35.
2   J. Noakes and G. Pridham, *Nazism: 1919-1945: Foreign Policy, War and Racial Extermination* (University of Exeter, 1988), p. 1199.
3   J. Forster, 'The Relation between Operation Barbarossa as an Ideological War of Extermination and the Final Solution' in D. Cesarini (ed.), *The Final Solution* (Routledge, 1994), p. 95.
4   D.J. Goldhagen, *Hitler's Willing Executioners: Ordinary Germans and the Holocaust* (Little, Brown and Company, 1996), p. 454.
5   J. Noakes and G. Pridham, *Nazism*, p. 1202.
6   Ibid, p. 574.
7   D.J. Goldhagen, *Hitler's Willing Executioners*, p. 9.
8   M. Marrus, *The Holocaust in History* (Penguin, 1989), p. 18.
9   W. Carr, *Hitler: A Study in Personality and Politics* (Edward Arnold, 1978), p. 114.
10 P. Burrin, *Hitler and the Jews: The Genesis of the Holocaust* (Edward Arnold, 1989), p. 150.

Answering essay questions on 'Conclusion: German Responsibility'

Consider the following questions:
1. To what extent were the German people 'Hitler's willing executioners'?
2. 'No Hitler: no Holocaust.' Do you agree?
3. 'A purely German enterprise' or 'An enterprise to which countless people throughout Europe contributed'. Which of these views of the Holocaust is more correct?

All three questions are concerned with the issue of responsibility for the Holocaust. But each is very different. You will need to consider the information from at least the last two chapters - and arguably the entire book - to have a reasonable stab at any one of them.

Construct an outline plan for question 1. First make a list of reasons to support the argument that the Germans were 'willing executioners'. Then make another list to support the view that they were not 'willing executioners'. (Section 6 should help!) Decide which line you are going to argue. (Remember it is not always good policy to sit on the fence.) Now compose an introductory paragraph of about seven or eight sentences. Next plan in rough seven or eight paragraphs. (Good essays often have this number.) What would each paragraph contain?

Let's move on to question 2. Brainstorm the kinds of information you would be including in the answer and how you might consider organising the material. Now write a conclusion (again of seven or eight sentences). In your conclusion you should be recapping, drawing together the threads of the argument and finally giving your opinion on the central issue in the set question. Your conclusion should not be loaded down with factual information. Nor should you spring some new and previously unexplored idea that you have just thought of on the reader. The conclusion should stem logically from the rest of the essay. Try to present a reasoned and balanced answer - and don't necessarily be persuaded by my viewpoint. Providing you can support your own view with sound evidence and display an awareness of the arguments of the other 'side', you have nothing to fear.

Now for question 3. Draw up a rough plan of seven or eight paragraphs. Now write an introduction and conclusion (each of seven or eight sentences). Imagine that an examiner only reads the introduction and conclusion. Does your introduction analyse the question? Does your conclusion present a good summary of the rest of the planned essay? Do your introduction and conclusion together go a long way to answering the set question? If not, think of ways you could improve matters. If so, remember to use the successful formula in future essays.

Summary Diagram
Conclusion: German Responsibility

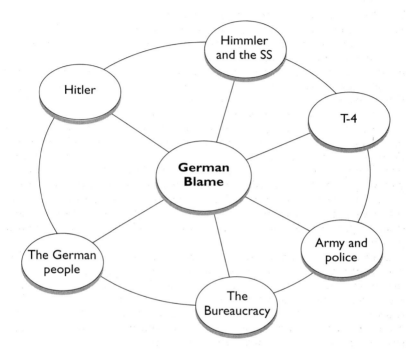

Chronological Table

1889	April	Hitler's birth.
1907-1913		Hitler in Vienna.
1913		Hitler moved to Munich.
1914	August	Start of the First World War.
1918	November	End of the First World War.
1919	January	Setting up of the Weimar Republic.
	September	Hitler joined the German Workers' Party.
1920		Formation of the National Socialist German Workers' Party.
1923	November	Beer Hall Putsch.
1925		First volume of *Mein Kampf* published.
1929		Start of the Great Depression.
1930		Nazi breakthrough in Reichstag elections.
1932	July	Nazis became the strongest single party in Germany.
1933	January	Hitler appointed German Chancellor.
	February	Acts of violence against Jews and Jewish shops by Nazis.
	March	The Nazis and the Nationalists won a majority in the Reichstag.
	March	Enabling Law passed.
	March	First concentration camp at Dachau set up.
	April	First official boycott of Jewish firms.
	April	Law for the Restoration of the Professional Civil Service.
	April	Law against Overcrowding of German Schools and Universities.
	October	Editorial law excluded German Jews from the press.
1934	June	'Night of the Long Knives'.
	July	SS became an independent organisation within the Nazi Party.
	August	Death of Hindenburg. Hitler now the Führer.
1935	Spring	Acts of violence by Nazis against Jews and Jewish shops.
	July	Registrars told not to solemnise 'mixed marriages'.
	September	Reich Citizenship Law and Law for the Protection of German Blood and German Honour - the Nuremberg Laws.
	November	First Ordinance to the Reich Citizenship Law.
1936	February	Winter Olympics staged in Germany.
	August	Summer Olympics staged in Germany.
1937	November	Schacht dismissed as Minister of Economics. Intensification of Aryanisation programme.
1938	March	Annexation of Austria (*Anschluss*).

	April	Registration of all Jews with assets exceeding 5,000 Reichsmark.
	October	Jewish passports to be stamped with a large J.
	October	17,000 Polish Jews in Germany are made 'stateless'.
	November	German diplomat von Rath murdered in Paris by a Polish Jew.
	November	*Kristallnacht.*
	November	Jews forced to pay compensation for *Kristallnacht.*
	November	Jews forbidden to visit theatres, cinemas, concerts etc.
	November	Expulsion of all Jewish pupils from schools.
	December	Compulsory closure and sale of all Jewish businesses.
1939	January	All Jews have to carry the middle name Israel or Sara.
	January	Heydrich to direct Reich Central Office for Jewish Emigration.
	January	Hitler's threatening Reichstag speech.
	March	German troops invaded Czechoslovakia.
	September	Germany attacked Poland: start of Second World War.
	September	Heydrich decree marked the start of ghettoisation in Poland.
	October	Hitler authorised the euthanasia programme.
	October	Himmler appointed Reich Commissar for the Strengthening of Germandom and given charge of all resettlement plans.
	November	Jews in General Government forced to wear yellow star of David.
	December	87,000 Poles and Jews deported from the Warthegau to the General Government.
1940	January	First experimental gassing of mental patients in German hospitals.
	April	Germany invaded Denmark and Norway.
	May	Germany invaded Holland and Belgium.
	June	France surrendered. Vichy government, led by Marshall Petain, set up.
	June	Foreign Office and RSHA start work on the Madagascar Plan.
	October	Jews from west Germany sent to camps in France.
	November	Warsaw ghetto 'sealed'.
1941	March	Hitler revealed to *Wehrmacht* commanders that the war against the USSR was to be a war of extermination.
	April	Army high command agreed to the operation of SS units in the rear army areas.

	June	Germany invaded USSR.
	June/July	*Einsatzgruppen* move into USSR behind the advancing armies.
	July	Goering ordered Heydrich to formulate a 'comprehensive solution to the Jewish problem'.
	August	Hitler ordered the official end to the euthanasia programme.
	September	All German Jews forced to wear the star of David.
	September	First experimental gassings of Soviet POWs at Auschwitz.
	September	Mass killing of Jews at Babi Yar, Kiev.
	October	First deportation order for Jews from the Reich.
	November	Mass killings of Jews in Riga.
	December	German declaration of war on USA.
	December	Gassing of Jews began at Chelmno.
1942	January	Wannsee Conference arranged the Final Solution.
	March	Gassings began at Belzec.
	April	Sobibor opened as a death camp.
	May	Start of mass gassings at Auschwitz.
	May	Assassination of Reinhard Heydrich.
	July	Start of deportation of Jews from the Warsaw ghetto to Treblinka.
	July	Start of mass deportation of Jews from western Europe to Auschwitz.
	September	Start of mass gassing at Majdanek.
	December	RSHA ordered deportation of all German Gypsies to Auschwitz.
1943	April	End of mass killings in Chelmno.
	April	Start of Warsaw ghetto uprising.
	May	End of Warsaw ghetto uprising.
	August	End of gassing at Treblinka.
	September	7,500 Danish Jews ferried to safety in Sweden.
	October	End of Operation Reinhard.
	November	Liquidation of Riga ghetto and killing of the remaining Jews in Majdanek.
1944	May	Start of deportations of Hungarian Jews to Auschwitz.
	June	Allied landings in Normandy.
	June	Start of transports and death marches of prisoners from Auschwitz to camps further west.
	November	Himmler ordered end of gassings.
1945	January	Soviet troops liberated Auschwitz.
	April	German and Austrian concentration camps liberated by the Allies.
	April	Hitler committed suicide.
	May	Nazi Germany surrendered.

Glossary

Aktion T-4	Co-ordinated the euthanasia programme: T-4 after address of central office in Berlin at Tiergartenstrasse 4.
Anschluss	Annexation of Austria in March 1938.
Barbarossa	German plan to attack the USSR.
Einsatzgruppen	Special force: SS and police killing units.
Einsatzkommando	Special unit - an individual detachment of an *Einsatzgruppen*.
Final Solution	Short version of Nazi term: 'Final Solution of the Jewish Question' - a euphemism for the programme to exterminate European Jewry.
Führer	The Leader (Adolf Hitler).
Führer Chancellery	Hitler's own personal chancellery that handled his personal affairs and a number of specially assigned policies.
Gau	Regional Party district.
Gauleiter	Regional Party leader.
General Government	The Nazi-ruled state in central and eastern Poland during the Second World War - headed by Hans Frank.
Gestapo	Secret state police.
Holocaust	Post-war term for the murder of some 6 million Jews.
Judenrat	Jewish council.
Kristallnacht	Literally 'night of broken glass': Nazi-organised pogrom - 9-10 November 1938.
Lebensraum	Living space: Nazi metaphor for the desire to expand in eastern Europe.
Mischlinge	Persons of partly Jewish descent.
Ostland	The Nazi administrative unit comprising the conquered territories of Estonia, Latvia, Lithuania and Byelorussia.
RKFD	Reich Commissar for the Strengthening of Germandom (ie Himmler).
RSHA	Reich Security Main Office: formed in 1939 under Heydrich. Its departments included the *Gestapo*, the criminal police and the SD.
SA	*Stürmabteilung* (Storm troopers).
SD	Security service - the SS intelligence agency.
Sonderkommando	Special detail of prisoners.
SS	*Schutzstaffel:* (defence echelon) The elite Nazi organisation run by Heinrich Himmler.
Völkisch	Racial-nationalist.
Warthegau	Territory in western Poland annexed by Germany after its conquest of Poland.
Wehrmacht	The German armed forces.

Further Reading

You will not be surprised to learn that there are hundreds of excellent books on the Holocaust - especially by British, American, German and Israeli historians. This list offers only a brief sample of some of the most significant works. It is unlikely that you will have time to consult more than just a few of these. However, it is vital that you read some, particularly if you are taking the topic as a special or depth study. The topic is one of considerable controversy and you will be in a better position to form your own conclusions if you have read widely. The following suggestions are meant to serve as a guide.

1 General Texts

There are many general works that cover anti-Semitism and the Holocaust. R. Hilberg, *The Destruction of the European Jews* (Holmes and Meier, 1985) remains a classic. L. Dawidowicz, *The War Against the Jews 1933-1945* (Penguin, 1990) and G. Fleming, *Hitler and the Final Solution* (University of California Press, 1985) are powerful statements of the intentionalist case. M. Marrus, *The Holocaust in History* (Penguin, 1989) provides a lucid exposition of the rival interpretations from the 1970s to the late 1980s.

M. Gilbert, *The Holocaust: A History of the Jews in Europe during the Second World War* (Rinehart and Winston, 1985) contains a wealth of detail. M. Gilbert, *Atlas of the Holocaust* (Michael Joseph, 1982) has some excellent maps. Try also L. Yahil, *The Holocaust: The Fate of European Jewry, 1932-1945* (Oxford University Press, 1990) - a mammoth work, and P. Burrin, *Hitler and the Jews: The Genesis of the Holocaust* (Arnold, 1994) - a succinct overview of the processes that led to the Final Solution. I. Gutman (ed), *Encyclopedia of the Holocaust* (Macmillan, 1990) is invaluable. So is D. Cesarani (ed), *The Final Solution: Origins and Implementation* (Routledge, 1996) - a splendid collection of essays by many of the key Holocaust scholars.

2 Anti-Semitism

There are a number of good books on the European and German background to anti-Semitism. L. Poliakov, *A History of Anti-Semitism* 4 Vols (Oxford University Press, 1965-1986) provides an immensely detailed but also analytical history of anti-Semitism. J. Katz, *From Prejudice to Destruction: Anti-Semitism, 1700-1933* (CUP, 1980) provides a shorter but still very comprehensive overview.

3 Nazism

There are a colossal number of texts on Hitler and Nazi Germany. These are some of my favourites: W. Carr, *Hitler: A Study in Personality and Politics* (Arnold, 1978) - still an excellent introduction to many of the major debates about Hitler and the Nazi regime. A. Bullock, *Hitler and Stalin: Parallel Lives* (Alfred A. Knopf, 1992) and A. Bullock, *Hitler: A Study in Tyranny* (Penguin, 1962) are both classics. Try also I. Kershaw, *Hitler* (Longman, 1991). K.P. Fischer, *Nazi Germany* (Constable and Company, 1995) is a good one-volume text on the Third Reich, but G. Layton, *Germany: The Third Reich: 1933-1945* (Hodder and Stoughton, 1992) is probably more accessible. R.G.L. Waite, *The Psychopathic God* (Basic Books, 1977) provides an interesting (but for me unconvincing) psycho-historical dimension. R.F. Hamilton, *Who Voted for Hitler* (Princeton University Press, 1982) examines which Germans voted Nazi and why. I. Kershaw, *The Nazi Dictatorship: Problems and Perspectives* (Edward Arnold, 1985) is essential reading. See also I. Kershaw, *Popular Opinion and Political Dissent in the Third Reich: Bavaria, 1933-1945* (Oxford University Press, 1983). Michael Burleigh and Wolfgang Wippermann, *The Racial State: Germany 1933-1945* (CUP, 1991) could just as easily have been mentioned in the general text section.

4 Anti-Semitism in Action: 1933-9

The best recent book is S. Friedländer, *Nazi Germany and the Jews: The Years of Persecution 1933-39* (Weidenfeld and Nicolson,1997). See also K.A. Schleunes, *The Twisted Road to Auschwitz: Nazi Policies Toward the Jews, 1933-1939* (University of Illinois Press, 1970) and H. Graml, *Anti-Semitism in the Third Reich* (Blackwell, 1992). J. Noakes and G. Pridham (eds), *Nazism 1919-1945: 2: State, Economy and Society 1933-1939: A Documentary Reader* (University of Exeter, 1984) is a vital collection of texts, with brilliant commentaries.

5 The Effect of War: 1939-41 (and Euthanasia)

C.R. Browning, *The Path to Genocide* (CUP, 1992) is a useful collection of essays on the period 1939-41, especially the situation in the Polish ghettos. H. Friedländer, *The Origins of Nazi Genocide: From Euthanasia to the Final Solution* (University of North Carolina, 1995) is a fascinating study of the Nazi euthanasia programme, as is M.R. Burleigh, *Death and Deliverance: 'Euthanasia' in Germany 1900-1945* (CUP, 1994).

6 The Final Solution: 1941-5

R. Breitman, *The Architect of Genocide: Himmler and the Final Solution* (The Bodley Head, 1991) examines the career of the SS leader. G. Hirschfeld, *The Policies of Genocide: Jews and Soviet Prisoners of War in Nazi Germany* (Allen and Unwin, 1986) contains five important essays, including a vital one by Hans Mommsen, 'The Realization of the Unthinkable: The Final Solution of the Jewish Question in the Third Reich.' C.R. Browning, *Ordinary Men: Reserve Police Battalion 101 and the Final Solution in Poland* (HarperCollins, 1992) is also a must.

On the death camps see K.G. Feig, *Hitler's Death Camps* (Holmes and Meier, 1981) and Y. Arad, *Belzec, Sobibor and Treblinka: The Operation Reinhard Death Camps* (Indiana University Press, 1987).

J. Noakes and G. Pridham, *Nazism 1919-1945: Foreign Policy, War and Racial Extermination: A Documentary Reader* (University of Exeter, 1988) contains a tremendous collection of documents and equally tremendous commentary.

7 Who Was to Blame for the Holocaust?

See H. Arendt, *Eichmann in Jerusalem. A Report on the Banality of Evil* (Viking, 1963) for a criticism of Jewish leadership. I.Trunk, *Judenrat* (Macmillan, 1972) analyses the activity and constraints of the Jewish councils. E. Cohen, *Human Behaviour in the Concentration Camps* (Free Association Books, 1988) is a psychoanalytical study of camp behaviour. Y. Bauer, *They Chose Life: Jewish Resistance in the Holocaust* (American Jewish Committee, 1973) deals with Jewish resistance.

D.J. Goldhagen, *Hitler's Willing Executioners: Ordinary Germans and the Holocaust* (Little, Brown and Company, 1996) is a powerful indictment of the German people. See also R. Hilberg, *Perpetrators, Victims, Bystanders* (Harper Collins, 1992) and D. Bankier, *The Germans and the Final Solution: Public Opinion Under Nazism* (Blackwell, 1992). The following are more specific: G. Reitlinger, *The SS: Alibi of a Nation, 1922-1945* (Prentice-Hall, 1981); C.W. Snydor, *Soldiers of Destruction: The SS Death's Head Division, 1933-1945* (Princeton University Press, 1977); R. Gellately, *The Gestapo and German Society: Enforcing Racial Policy 1933-1945* (Clarendon Press, 1990); O. Bartov, *The Eastern Front, 1941-1945: German Troops and the Barbarization of Warfare* (Macmillan, 1985).

A. Morse, *While Six Million Died* (Random House, 1967) criticises the role played by the USA, as does D.S. Wyman, *The Abandonment of the Jews. America and the Holocaust 1941-1945* (Pantheon Books, 1984). M. Gilbert, *Auschwitz and the Allies* (Mandarin, 1991) examines the failure of the Allies to bomb Auschwitz in 1944. B. Wasserstein, *Britain and the Jews of Europe, 1935-1945* (Oxford University Press, 1979) examines the role played by Britain. W. Rubinstein, *The Myth of the Rescue* (Routledge, 1997), argues persuasively that there was little Britain or the USA could have done to rescue the Jews. S. Friedländer, *Pius X11 and the Third Reich: A Documentation* (Knopf, 1966) examines the role of the Vatican in the Holocaust.

8 Primary Material

J. Noakes and G. Pridham's *Nazism* series is an invaluable collection.

Other useful collections of documents include: L.S. Dawidowicz (ed), *A Holocaust Reader* (New York, 1976) and R. Hilberg (ed),

Documents of Destruction: Germany and Jewry, 1933-1945 (Quadrangle Books, 1971).

L. Dobroazycki (ed), *The Chronicle of the Lodz Ghetto 1941-1944* (Yale University Press, 1984) is an interesting read. I. Ehrenburg and V. Grossman (eds), *The Black Book* (Holocaust Library, 1981), contains sources on the destruction within the USSR. R. Hilberg (ed), T*he Warsaw Diary of Adam Czerniakow* (Stein and Day, 1979), is the diary of the Warsaw *Judenrat* leader who committed suicide on the eve of deportation. F. Muller, *Eyewitness Auschwitz* (Stein and Day, 1979), is a vivid survivor account, as is P. Levi, *Survival in Auschwitz* (Collier Books, 1958).

For the Nazi perspective try R. Hoess, *Commandant in Auschwitz* (World Publishing Co, 1959), and A. Hitler, *Mein Kampf* (Hutchinson, 1969). See also E. Klee, et al., *The Good Old Days: The Holocaust as Seen by its Perpetrators and Bystanders* (Free Press, 1991).

Y. Arad (ed), *The Pictorial History of the Holocaust* (Macmillan, 1990) contains some useful illustrations, as does Time-Life, *The Apparatus of Death* (Time-Life Books,1991).

9 Other

You really must read T. Keneally, *Schindler's List* (Penguin Books, 1983) or see the film/video.

Index

A selection of bestselling and related titles from Hodder & Stoughton *Educational*

Title	Author	ISBN	Price (UK)
Fascism and Nazism	Robert Pearce	0 340 67946 6	£6.50
From Bismarck to Hitler: Germany 1890-1933	Geoff Layton	0 340 59488 8	£6.50
Germany: The Third Reich 1933-45	Geoff Layton	0 340 53847 3	£6.50
War and Peace: International Relations 1914-45	David Williamson	0 340 57165 9	£6.50
Italy: Liberalism and Fascism 1870-1945	Mark Robson	0 340 54548 8	£6.50
Reactions and Revolutions: Russia 1881-1924	Michael Lynch	0 340 53336 6	£6.50

All Hodder & Stoughton *Educational* books are available from your local bookshop, or can be ordered direct from the publisher. Just tick the titles you would like and complete the details below. Prices and availablilty are subject to change without prior notice.

Please enclose a cheque or postal order made payable to *Bookpoint Limited,* and send to: Hodder & Stoughton *Educational*, 39 Milton Park, Abingdon, Oxon OX14 4TD, UK. EMail address: orders @bookpoint.co.uk

UK postage will be charged at £2.00 for each book plus £2.30 for packing. Four books and above will be charged at 5% of the invoice value (minimum charge £5.00).

If you would like to pay by credit card, our centre team would be delighted to take your order by telephone. Our direct line (44) 01235 400414 (lines open 9.00am - 6.00pm, Monday to Saturday, with a 24 hour answering service). Alternatively you could send a fax to (44) 01235 400454.

Title _____ First name _____ Surname _____

Address _____

_____

_____

Postcode _____ Daytime telephone no. _____

If you would prefer to pay by credit card, please complete:

Please debit my Master Card / Access / Diner's Card / American Express (delete as applicable)

Card number _____

Expiry date _____ Signature _____

If you would like to receive further information on our products, please tick the box ☐